BUILDING
& MOBILIZING TEAMS

Y★UTH MINISTRY IN THE TRENCHES

BUILDING

& MOBILIZING TEAMS

Y★UTH MINISTRY IN THE TRENCHES

Marv Penner

Standard®
PUBLISHING
Bringing The Word to Life

Cincinnati, Ohio

Published by Standard Publishing, Cincinnati, Ohio
www.standardpub.com

Copyright © 2009 by Marv Penner

Also available from the Youth Ministry in the Trenches series: *Engaging Parents as Allies* and *Reaching Unchurched Teens*

Printed in the United States of America

Project editor: Robert Irvin
Cover and interior design: Thinkpen Design, Inc., www.thinkpendesign.com

Series contributor: David Olshine

ISBN 978-0-7847-2316-6

Library of Congress Cataloging-in-Publication Data

Penner, Marv, 1951-
  Building & mobilizing teams / Marv Penner.
    p. cm. -- (Youth ministry in the trenches)
  Includes bibliographical references and index.
  ISBN 978-0-7847-2316-6 (perfect bound; hinge score: alk. paper)
  1. Church work with youth. 2. Group ministry. I. Title. II. Title: Building and mobilizing teams.
  BV4447.P368 2009
  259'.23--dc22
                              2009012643

15 14 13 12 11 10 09   9 8 7 6 5 4 3 2 1

CONTENTS

WHAT MAKES A GREAT TEAM?

I've had the privilege of serving on a whole lot of teams over the course of my life. They've included sports teams, drama teams, music teams, missions teams, leadership committees, church staffs, volunteer teams, planning groups, and I even spent five years as a member of a professional firefighting crew. In some cases, I had the privilege of leading the team. In others, I was one of the followers. Some of the teams I've worked with accomplished their goals flawlessly. Others, like our seminary faculty intramural hockey team of 1998, flopped miserably. (What did a bunch of biblical scholars and one youth ministry prof think would happen?)

All that makes for a lot of memories. In fact, as I look back I can probably say I've had some of my very best, and some of my very worst, ministry experiences in the context of a team. As I sat down to write this book, I took some time to reflect on all those experiences and tried to think about the specific factors that distinguished the good teams from the bad teams and the bad from the ugly. There are some clear patterns . . .

Shared purpose: One of the factors common to every positive team experience I've had is that each member of the team was committed to the same desired outcome. That meant everyone was pulling in the same direction with a clear sense of why we were doing what we were doing. In situations where the purpose was unclear or, even worse, when multiple agendas were being pursued, the benefit of the team was lost. I've even been on some teams where differing desired outcomes were actually in direct competition with one another. It doesn't get much worse than that.

Equal levels of commitment: Is there anything as frustrating as being fired up to get a job done, and done well, but at the same time being stuck on a team with a bunch of people who couldn't care less? Think back to that science fair project when you got partnered with those three losers who just wanted to plant seeds in Styrofoam cups while you had visions of creating a nuclear reactor. The truth of the matter is that in most team situations some individuals will be more highly motivated than others at various points along the way. If you find the apathy of a few team members is dragging down the energy of the whole team, it's generally better to give those few members the opportunity to step aside before they derail the whole process. When the whole team has the same objective and each member gives himself or herself fully to the task, everyone has a great time.

Open, honest communication: This is about creating an environment where people are free to express their thoughts, ideas, opinions, concerns, critiques, beliefs, and feelings. I've served on some teams where it was dangerous to suggest any ideas that were different from those of the leader. On that kind of team, everyone is cautious, measured, and guarded. The political pecking order is clearly established and the lower that people are in that order, the less they're able to contribute. The kind of openness I'm talking about here requires a high level of trust in one another and in a leader who establishes an ethos of collaboration and equality.

A bit of play time: Task groups can become so focused on their goals that the whole effort ends up being no fun to be part of. However, a healthy mix of social interaction and focused work makes a team more than just a machine grinding away to get a job done. The teams I've truly enjoyed being a part of were those where actual friendships were formed in the process of achieving the goals. For fourteen years I had the privilege of being on a church pastoral staff that laughed and cried together, worked and played together, sat together in the boardroom and sat together at the restaurant, made important decisions about the future of our church and made important decisions about which club to use when standing over the next tough shot on the golf course. That group stands alone as one of the best teams I've ever experienced.

A great leader: Great groups usually have great leaders. I could spend the rest of this book telling stories about some of the weak, insecure, arrogant, driven, self-serving, passionless, condescending, and bullheaded leaders I've had the opportunity to observe—but that would only serve to be negative. Instead, I'm choosing to think about leaders who were godly, generous, humble, collaborative, open, and servant-hearted. These are leaders who have given me the sense that my contribution is valued and that my voice is heard. These are leaders who are willing to accept responsibility when things go wrong and share the applause when things go right. These are leaders who are able to keep the group on task without having to resort to the use of power. These are the kinds of leaders we want to become.

Acknowledgments

This book is all about building and mobilizing teams for effective youth ministry in the trenches. It's written to those who are called to guide teams of student leaders and adult volunteers in the crucial task of pointing a young generation to a growing relationship with Jesus. I can't think of a more significant task. Everything I've just said about what makes for a good team applies to the world of youth ministry.

Whether you're a volunteer who heads up the youth ministry in your church or you get paid as a staff member, the principles are the same, as are the challenges. I trust you'll find this book to be more practical than philosophical and that some of the suggestions you'll encounter in these pages will strengthen you as a leader and strengthen your team. You've been given the high calling of representing Jesus to the students he has entrusted to your care.

Most everything I've learned about team play has come from two sources: the gifted and godly leaders I've had the privilege of working under—Tic Long, John Wilkinson, Arnold Reimer, to name a few; and the hundreds of incredible volunteers I've had the privilege of shepherding over the years. As I wrote this book my mind was constantly flooded with great memories of work that was accomplished together in a spirit of friendship, shared vision, laughter, and great joy. Thanks for teaching me everything that's good about teams.

And a special thanks to Bob Irvin and all the folks at Standard Publishing for making this a most pleasant project. I'm honored to be part of your team.

Dedication

This book is dedicated to my son Jeff. You have volunteered with humility and dedication on so many teams over the years. You never needed the spotlight, always working faithfully, often behind the scenes. Now you are being asked to lead and I can't tell you how proud of you I am. As you lead with the same servant spirit that I've seen in you through your whole life, I'm confident God will use you to accomplish great things for his sake. I know you'll hear it one day, but on this side of Heaven let your dad be the one to say, "Well done, good and faithful servant."

Marv Penner

LAKE COUNTY, BC, CANADA

PART ONE

THINKING
IT THROUGH

THINKING ABOUT TEAMS

Vienna, Austria, is unmistakably, unapologetically a musical mecca. Walking the heart of this beautifully preserved European city makes you feel like you could bump into Mozart or Brahms around any corner. In fact, the timeless melodies of these two geniuses ring up and down the ancient avenues from the cellos, French horns, clarinets, flutes, and harpsichords of incredibly gifted young musicians overheard practicing behind open windows or busking in the streets for some loose change. It's classical music heaven.

The main city square crawls with men and women dressed in the costumes of yesteryear. The knee-length knickers and ruffles, white curled wigs, and long silk cuffs are all part of a carefully crafted tourist trade designed to cash in on the history of this incredible city. The task of these time-traveling marketers is to sell tickets for the countless classical musical performances that take place throughout the city every evening.

On a recent visit to the city, I couldn't pass up the opportunity to take in one of those concerts, even though, after more than thirty years in youth ministry, I prefer a good mosh pit to a string quintet. But hey! . . . when in Rome—or in this case, Vienna—you've got to do as the locals do. To miss one of these would be like going to New York and not taking a late night stroll through Times Square . . . or visiting Australia and not seeing a kangaroo . . . or stopping in Cawker City, Kansas, and missing the world's biggest ball of twine. There are some things in life that are clearly not optional.

Before the afternoon was done I had caved and negotiated with a Louis XIV look-alike for a ticket to what actually turned out to be an unbelievable musical extravaganza—a full orchestra, elaborate costumes, beautiful ballerinas, great comedy, and all of it happening in a stunning old castle that oozed history out of every nook and cranny. It was a spectacular performance. Who would've thought Mozart could be that much fun?

When I stepped back out into the cool Austrian evening, I felt like I had gotten more than my money's worth. As I headed back toward the city square—the harmonies still fresh in my memory—I was feeling pretty great. And that's when I heard them. A frantic harmonica backed up by a slightly out-of-tune guitar. Cymbals and drums not quite keeping up. A banjo picking up the melody, such as it was, where the guitar had left off. Horns and whistles inserted randomly into the chaotic cacophony. The melody was unmistakably Mozart, but where had these people learned to play? It was only when I turned the corner and bumped into a crowd of tourists that I saw what I had been hearing. It wasn't *them*. It was *him*.

An old leather-faced guy with a beat-up guitar hung around his neck and a banjo slung over his back. A harmonica clamped in a wire vice hovered in front of his grinning lips. Under each elbow were a couple of horns he might have stolen off some poor kid's bike. Between his knees were a set of cymbals and at each foot three or four pedals that were rigged to work a wild collection of percussion instruments. A xylophone stood there waiting for its turn and a rack held an insane variety of things that made noises when you blew into them. It was a musical car wreck; you couldn't help but stop and stare. Knees banging, feet stomping, hands alternately strumming and grabbing one bizarre instrument after another. I must say, it was impressive—a chaotic, messy, frenzied kind of impressive. But this man wasn't doing his native city any favors. That's just not how music is done in Vienna.

The contrast between what I had enjoyed in the concert hall and what I was experiencing on the street was astounding. The orchestra was committed to working together to create its carefully crafted harmonies, while the street clown was trying to do it all by himself. At some level, I suppose one could say, he was getting the job done. But this isn't the way it was meant to be.

This book is all about doing youth ministry as a team, as it was meant to be done. When it comes to doing ministry—especially with teenagers—there is simply no substitute for putting together a solid, diverse team and using its breadth of energy, ideas, relational strength, and spiritual influence to reach a generation. It's just not a gig for a one-man band.

Maybe you aren't a musician, and the orchestra metaphor doesn't work for you. Then think about a well-coached athletic squad with each of the positions being played for the purpose of strengthening the team as a whole. The offensive linemen who open up a hole for the running back to blast through. The volleyball setter who softly lays the ball at the top of the net to set up the power hitter for a hammering attack. The shortstop flipping the ball to the second baseman, who fires it to first for a perfect double play. A great team that plays *together* gets the job done.

TRUTH FROM THE TRENCHES

When it comes to doing ministry—especially ministry with teenagers—there is simply no substitute for putting together a solid, diverse team and using its breadth of energy, ideas, relational strength, and spiritual influence to reach a generation. It's simply not a one-man job.

Or perhaps you can visualize a military platoon where each of the soldiers is literally responsible for the life and safety of the others as they live out their mission. Each role has been carefully rehearsed during years of training because the stakes are so high. When that well-oiled machine kicks into gear, everyone knows exactly what his job is. The stakes are high, but with everyone committed to a common purpose and with each person looking out for the others, it's amazing what can be accomplished.

The metaphor you choose doesn't really matter, but the connections to the way we do youth ministry should be obvious. A lone ranger approach to youth ministry is like a one-man band—it's not the way God meant things to be.

The goal of youth ministry is actually quite straightforward, but the process by which it is accomplished requires the very best of all of us. After years of thinking it through and making it work with the teams I've led, this is a generic mission statement I've come up with to describe the ministry of a youth worker:

Through shared experiences and modeling friendships with spiritually mature adults, young people are invited into a growing relationship with Christ and into greater conformity with his character.

We're talking about a journey. Our work involves accompanying a generation on its journey from childhood to adulthood and helping young people discover the life they were intended to live along the way. It's a treacherous path filled with challenges and plagued with potential distractions that often sabotage the outcomes. In fact, Ephesians 6 tells us we're in a battle with spiritual forces that we may not even be consciously aware of. It's not a battle to be taken on alone.

We've talked a bit about orchestras, sports teams, and armies. But God's word has plenty to say about the importance of working as a team as well. Perhaps the most powerful picture the Bible gives us to describe how we were meant to function is that of the human body; it's described in 1 Corinthians 12.

> *Now the body is not made up of one part but of many. If the foot should say, "Because I am not a hand, I do not belong to the body," it would not for that reason cease to be part of the body. And if the ear should say, "Because I am not an eye, I do not belong to the body," it would not for that reason cease to be part of the body. If the whole body were an eye, where would the sense of hearing be? If the whole body were an ear, where would the sense of smell be? But in fact God has arranged the parts in the body, every one of them, just as he wanted them to be. If they were all one part, where would the body be? As it is, there are many parts, but one body.*
>
> 1 CORINTHIANS 12:14-20

This familiar passage reminds us of the need to function in cooperation with one another for the purpose of achieving a larger goal. It speaks elegantly of our interconnectedness and interdependence. What Paul is trying to communicate to his friends in Corinth is that we were never meant to function in isolation. There is deep fulfillment when we function in a relationship that is marked by both giving and receiving. The body works best when each part gives way to the other and recognizes the value of each other part. The passage actually says that even if we wanted to declare independence, we would find that it's not our call to make. The key to understanding this biblical analogy is to grasp that God has arranged the parts to work together perfectly under his headship. Collaboration within the community of faith is not optional.

Unfortunately, in a lot of youth ministries, these basic biblical principles are simply not applied. It should make us wonder why.

TRUTH FROM THE TRENCHES

God has arranged the parts of the body—and any healthy ministry team—to work together perfectly under his headship. Collaboration within the community of faith is not optional.

ACTION PLAN

★ What are some of the best team experiences you've ever had?

★ What made those experiences so positive?

THINKING ABOUT THE ATTRACTIVENESS OF LONE RANGER MINISTRY

Most youth ministry leaders intuitively understand the value of working with a team. They know their ministry effectiveness will be increased and more students will have their relational needs met if ministry responsibility is spread broadly. Why, then, do so many of us in youth ministry continue to do our work alone? What are the lies that are easy for us to believe?

Here are a few of the reasons for the lone ranger mistakes we make that I've observed through the years. In the interest of full disclosure, I should let you know that I've been personally guilty of each of these at various points along my ministry journey.

'NO ONE IS WILLING TO HELP'

This may be the number one reason I hear from youth workers who continue to do their work alone. "I keep asking for help," they say. "But no one comes forward to help me." While there may be an element of truth to this in some churches and ministry organizations, to me it's clear that too many of us hide behind this excuse far too often. A pathetic "poor me" approach motivates no one, neither the lonely youth worker himself or herself, nor anyone else who might possibly consider joining in. There are appropriate ways to address this challenge. Later in this book, we'll deal with specific strategies for building a team in circumstances where recruitment is a challenge. But for now let me suggest that, for starters, an entirely different philosophical approach might be necessary. Instead of approaching the congregation like a pleading beggar with dozens of ministry slots to fill and plenty of guilt trips to dole out if people don't cooperate, what might happen if you turn this approach upside down?

What if you saw your role as that of the ministry facilitator rather than a headhunter desperately trying to get a name beside every job slot that needs filled? An aggressive recruitment approach creates an adversarial environment where people feel they need to defend themselves against the constant barrage of demands being made by leaders in the church. Instead, imagine an environment in which you as a leader offer to help every member of your spiritual community find a place to serve that is compatible with their gifts, passions, and abilities. This approach reinforces the notion that every believer should be expressing his or her ministry gifts in meaningful acts of service to the church and community—and in the process presents a very different tone regarding ministry.

Obviously, this plan requires us to trust God in some new ways as he puts together the various ministry teams that will work together to serve our congregations and communities. It may seem like a minor variation in direction, but the response it gets can be dramatically different. Of course, there are various practical ways to address this excuse and we'll deal with them specifically in part three (Making It Work).

POOR TIME MANAGEMENT

Even when there are people available, some leaders simply can't seem to get anyone to join them. It takes a lot of time and effort to put together a high-quality, efficient team. Involving a group of people to accomplish a task together takes preparation, careful planning, and strong communication. For some of us in youth ministry, these are foreign words. When we're flying by the seat of our pants we're in survival mode, and the effort it takes to bring others on board is simply too great. Examples: planning the games for a gym night on the way over to the gym means I'll have to lead them myself. Pulling together a Bible study the night before the group meets means it will be pretty tough to prepare the small group leaders for the discussion groups that should follow.

What we often forget is that with some advance planning and thoughtful delegation we can actually reduce the pressures of constantly being in survivor mode. Even if we've been able to recruit some people to help us, they likely won't last long on our team if we routinely operate a frantic, last-minute program.

INSECURITY AND APPLAUSE ADDICTION

Sometimes, in our desperate desire to be needed, we find ourselves unwilling to share the joy of ministry with others. We need the recognition and affirmation that comes from a job well done and we simply don't want to share the spotlight with anyone else. This approach to ministry not only robs others of the joy of participation, it reduces the effectiveness of everything we're trying to accomplish. Of course, anything in ministry that is done with the short-term goal of personal applause will end up feeling hollow and lifeless and in the end only create more pressure for us.

TRUTH FROM THE TRENCHES

Anything in ministry that is done with the short-term goal of personal applause will end up feeling hollow and lifeless and in the end only create more pressure for us.

LAZINESS AND/OR LACK OF VISION

This one is tough to face. A godly leader will always have the desire to see his or her scope of ministry increase—not for the sake of bigger numbers and the affirmation that might come from those numbers, but for the sake of seeing more and more young people touched by the truth of the gospel. When the vision for what could be is absent, a leader will have little motivation to grow a team and, with it, a ministry.

"We like it small and intimate," is one statement I often hear from leaders who are in this place. "If it ain't broke, don't fix it." I'm not assuming that a small youth group is broken, and just for the record I'm all for small and intimate as well. But the way to achieve healthy growth is to ensure that there are plenty of leaders who can share the relational responsibility as a group grows. Ask God to give you a vision for what your ministry could become; spend time in prayer on this specific point. Commit yourself to developing depth in the quality of relationships you have with your students and leave the issue of breadth to God. Just don't intentionally stifle growth by doing it all alone because of your lack of faith, which results in a lack of vision.

TRUTH FROM THE TRENCHES

Commit yourself to developing depth in the quality of relationships you have with your students; God will take care of the issue of growth and begin to give you vision for your ministry.

BASIC SELFISHNESS

Let's be real: there is great satisfaction and pleasure in doing youth ministry well. The relationships we cultivate with students can be deeply enjoyable. They share their lives and secrets with us, we walk with them through the crazy ups and downs of their adolescence, and we watch them respond to spiritual truth as it radically transforms their lives. And frankly, too often, we just don't want anybody else horning in on our happy little party. We love being the most important adult in the lives of our students.

This hoarding approach that some youth workers take could be the single biggest killer of youth ministry effectiveness. Don't let selfishness keep you from sharing the joy of ministry with others.

You might have been able to relate to some of these excuses for solo ministry. But if we really want to challenge the distorted thinking that's represented in the excuses we've just explored, we need to understand the benefits that come when we build our team and do ministry the way it was meant to be done.

ACTION PLAN

★ Do you struggle with any of the five reasons for solo ministry explored in this chapter? Be honest. How will you change any lone ranger mentality you're holding on to?

THINKING ABOUT THE BENEFITS OF WORKING AS A TEAM

Putting a healthy, well-functioning youth ministry team together requires a significant expenditure of time and energy, as we'll discover later in this book. But the dividends that are paid as a result literally set such a commitment apart as one of the best organizational investments you'll ever make. There are good reasons why Jesus built a team of twelve disciples around himself. Paul was extremely intentional in how he invested in those who would lead the churches he planted on his missionary journeys, and his letters are filled with references to relationships in numerous churches (Romans 16 is just one chapter that serves as an example). When the early church put together its leadership structures, the concept of team was central as the qualifications and roles of elders and deacons were carefully defined and managed. In short, the idea of doing ministry as community is well documented and illustrated throughout Scripture.

Let's talk about some practical ways your youth ministry will benefit when you get laser-focused about building and maintaining a healthy team to share in the opportunities and responsibilities of caring for the young people in your community.

IT GENERATES SYNERGY—OR, 2 + 3 = 7

The basic notion of *synergy* is that when you bring two or more forces together their combined outcome is often greater than the sum of the individual parts.

If that sounds a little mysterious and convoluted it's because it is. We are probably more familiar with the experience of it than the technicalities. Imagine that you're one of several people trying to solve the same problem or address the same dilemma. Working in isolation, each person views the issue from his or her own point of view and begins to work toward a solution. Compare this scenario to one in which three or four of you gather together at one table and address a problem collaboratively. Suddenly, the liveliness of the conversation, the diversity of points of view, and the opportunity to respond to one another's thinking generates a level of energy that never could have been achieved if the individuals had been left to work on the problem alone. This is synergy and it's a common experience when teams work together to accomplish kingdom purposes. In many cases the outcomes of a team brainstorming or planning session can lead to ministry ideas and dreams that likely never would have been generated if one person was trying to do it alone.

IT COMPENSATES FOR THE HUMANNESS OF INDIVIDUAL TEAM MEMBERS

As the saying goes, some people are just a little less perfect than others. My wife and kids remind me of this on a regular basis. There is simply no doubt that each of us brings our own weaknesses, preconceived ideas, personal baggage, relationally destructive patterns, and plain old sinfulness to the teams we're part of. The beauty of having a team is that often the weaknesses of one individual can be balanced by a strength that another person brings.

In the 1 Corinthians passage that compares the church to the human body, we read about parts that appear to be weaker, less honorable, and even unpresentable (1 Corinthians 12:21-23). But Paul goes on to indicate that the weaker parts are actually indispensable, the less honorable parts are given special honor, and that even the unpresentable parts are carefully protected, with modesty and respect. Each part has a role to play and when one of those parts fails to make a contribution, the whole body loses.

> The eye cannot say to the hand, "I don't need you!" And the head cannot say to the feet, "I don't need you!" On the contrary, those parts of the body that seem to be weaker are indispensable, and the parts that we think are less honorable we treat with special honor. And the parts that are unpresentable are treated with special modesty.
>
> 1 CORINTHIANS 12:21-23

One of the myths about Christianity is that in order for the body to work well we all need to be "balanced" people. I don't think anything could be further from the truth. The more "balanced" all of us are the more beige and boring the body becomes. God created each of us as unique and even imbalanced individuals. He seems to find great joy in putting together the most bizarre combinations of eccentric, off-balance people and then, out of all that uniqueness, creating a balance that perfectly matches his purposes.

I'm reminded of a married couple that volunteered to work with our senior high students. The husband was insanely competitive and was able to turn any activity into a contest where someone would win and someone would lose. On winter retreats we couldn't just ride tubes down the hill—he'd bring out a stopwatch. Sitting around the campfire with him on a canoe trip quickly turned into a competition in who could hold their breath the longest, who could eat the most hot dogs in three minutes, or who could beat him in an arm wrestle—"Come on, you wimps. I'll use my left arm!" Some of the kids loved it and tried to outdo him with competitions they would invent (some of which, in retrospect, probably could've gotten us sued), but others found all this irritating and disruptive. They didn't want to be in competitions every minute. That's where his wife came in. She was the most laid-back, chillaxed human being you could hope to find. There was nothing she loved more than to find a quiet spot down on the beach or near a fireplace where she would hang out, knit, and talk to kids by the hour. They compensated wonderfully for each other's extreme personalities, and our team was stronger because both of them were there.

You might be someone who feels weak in the area of creativity and new ideas but has strong listening skills and the spiritual gifts of mercy and hospitality. What a loss it would be to your team if you allowed your weakness to disqualify you from using the gifts God gave you to serve him. As God forms your team, he will likely bring someone along who can make up for your weaknesses, and someone else will benefit immensely from the strength that you bring to compensate for theirs.

DIVERSITY OF NEED CALLS FOR DIVERSITY ON THE TEAM

The individual stories that students bring to our small groups, Sunday school classes, and youth group events are so unique and diverse. Some kids come from great families that are genuinely as solid as they look. Others come from the most horrible brokenness we can imagine. Some are brand-new believers, some are bored and cynical because they've spent their whole lives around the church, and still others don't even know who Jesus is. Some like rock 'n' roll and others prefer country. Some are skaters and some are jocks. Some are withdrawn and timid while others are outgoing and confident. Some are quietly artistic and creative and some can't draw a convincing stickman. Some are streetwise and savvy while others are prudish and naive. Are you getting the idea?

There is no way that one individual can possibly meet the range of needs that a typically diverse group of teenagers represents. It doesn't matter how gifted you are or how relationally skilled you've become, you simply can't connect with every kid who comes through the door of your youth group. If we want to attract a diverse cross section of the adolescent population in our community or neighborhood into our ministries, we must intentionally offer a diverse team of relational adults.

Unfortunately, even when teams are intentionally put together, they too often represent very little by way of diversity. Five or six volunteers who are essentially clones of one another will attract a group of students that is equally homogeneous. It's important for us to recruit a team, but not just any team. Intentionally pursuing diversity in the team we put together will attract a broader range of students and create the opportunity for even broader ministry.

IT PREVENTS BURNOUT

All three of my kids are jugglers. When we get together for a family barbecue in the backyard, it doesn't take long before all sorts of objects are flying through the air. I'm not just talking about generic balls and clubs. I'm talking about flaming torches, machetes, eggs, bowling balls, and anything else they can get their hands on. It was interesting to watch each of them learn to juggle as they grew up. It always started with a basic cascade pattern that put three balls in that familiar circular motion. Once that simple pattern was mastered they began to add fancy moves—behind the back, under the leg, catch one of the balls with the back of your neck . . . but all still with three balls. Soon balls gave way to clubs and, in time, the bizarre array of objects I described above. The biggest challenges seemed to come not when switching from one kind of juggling object to another, but when they attempted to go from three to four and finally to five flying objects. For my kids that was the limit. Apparently there are people who can do ten or twelve balls at a time, but even they reach their limit at some point.

Juggling relationships is the same way: eventually, a capacity is reached. And when it is—and then that limit is exceeded—a subtle but relentless journey toward burnout begins.

Exodus chapter 18 records the story of a leader who was trying to manage more relationships than were humanly possible. It's an account that is packed with truth and well worth a careful read for any of us who serve as leaders. Moses was in the midst of the forty-year journey from Egypt to the promised land and the challenge of dealing with all the people under his care was obviously starting to wear on him. Apparently, Moses had sent his wife and two sons back home to live with Jethro, her father. The Bible doesn't explain exactly why this decision was made, but based on the rest of the passage I have a hunch that Moses just had way too much stuff going on to take good care of his family. The responsibility of leadership seemed to be overwhelming and it may be that there was just no energy left to invest in those who were closest to him. (Can you relate?)

In would appear that, at some point, Jethro decided it was time for the family to be reunited. So he packed up his daughter and her two sons and headed over to where Moses and all the people were. Moses spent the rest of that day telling his father-in-law all the amazing things he had been involved in. It was obviously a remarkable evening of stories; Jethro was clearly impressed (vv. 8-12).

The next day, Moses took up his familiar position again. He sat in his judging chair from morning until evening (v. 13) as people came to him with their squabbles and disputes so he could declare the proper verdicts. It was an Old Testament version of a *Judge Judy* marathon—stolen goats, noisy neighbors, borrowed sandals that hadn't been returned, people not picking up after their dogs . . . No doubt, as the day wore on, Jethro simply sat quietly and watched.

I can only imagine what must have been going through Moses' mind as he heard story after story and made one wise decision after another. *Hey, father-in-law.*

Look at me working my wisdom. Aren't you glad your daughter married the likes of me? Look how smart I am. Look how hard I work. I'm so happy to have you here for the day so you can see what a high-quality son-in-law you got in me.

But Jethro was not impressed (v. 14). He recognized that Moses was approaching his leadership responsibilities in a way that was ultimately going to destroy him and his family forever. Moses probably realized that he was in over his head, but like many of us, the pattern was too deeply entrenched to change. There wasn't time to implement a Plan B. He was just too busy working Plan A.

Of course, Jethro, a wise and seasoned leader, knew there was another way the job could be done. His suggestion was for Moses to identify a group of capable, godly, servant-hearted men to be trained and empowered to become judges in the community. He realized there were still some cases that would be so complex that they would require a higher court, but so much of what Moses was doing could have been done by a well-trained team that was given authority to act (vv. 17-23). Moses took his father-in-law's advice and, by the end of this episode, we see Jethro heading back home without his daughter and grandsons. He leaves them with Moses, knowing that now that the work has been delegated, Moses might have some time to invest in what really matters.

You may have heard an exhausted workaholic say, "It's better to burn out than rust out!" I'm afraid I have to disagree. Either way you're out! The best strategy is to create a healthy rhythm of work and rest that will allow you to stay in ministry over the long haul.

TRUTH FROM THE TRENCHES

You must delegate (Exodus 18). Among other reasons, it will help facilitate a personal, healthy rhythm of work and rest that will allow you to stay in ministry over the long haul.

SAFETY AND ACCOUNTABILITY

I recently heard the story of a volunteer youth worker whose once-small ministry began to grow. In spite of the fact that there were now more kids attending than he could adequately care for, he continued to carry the ministry by himself. As a single guy, he didn't have a lot of other family obligations to tie him down, so he poured himself wholeheartedly into caring for the youth group. Most of his social relationships were with teenagers. He didn't have a lot of time left in his busy week to maintain healthy friendships with people his own age. His house had an open-door policy, so teens felt free to come and go as they pleased. I bet you already know where this story is going; you're right. On a sleepover that he planned for his high school boys, things got carried away, the youth worker crossed some moral lines, there were accusations that several of the young boys were sexually assaulted, and a community and congregation were left devastated.

One of the important safeguards a team provides is the accountability of having several people present at every level of youth ministry. Solo youth workers are often left vulnerable because there is no one there to provide them with appropriate checks and balances. Obviously, the outcomes don't have to be as devastating as the story I've just shared with you to be significant. Further, no matter how small a youth group might be, it's important that both genders are represented in the leadership. Girls need a woman to go to and guys need healthy male role models who they can talk with about guy stuff. If only one of the genders is available, overall ministry effectiveness will immediately be reduced and potential risk increases.

Consider the youth worker who plans a wide-ranging game that consists of a number of dangerous elements. He's got kids running through an unfamiliar forest in the near-dark, climbing to high places without the right equipment and supervision, and building fires as part of the game's plot. Because of his own high tolerance for risk, it doesn't occur to him that his activity might be putting his students in danger. Another youth worker in the mix might look at the plan, recognize the dangers, ask some important questions, and ultimately save a group of students from potential harm.

TRUTH FROM THE TRENCHES

It's important that both genders are represented in your leadership. Girls need a woman to go to and guys need healthy male role models who they can talk with about guy stuff. If only one gender is available? Ministry effectiveness is reduced and risk increases.

What about the Bible study leader who writes his own curriculum reflecting a distorted understanding of Scripture and then teaches young students his perspective with great authority? The potential dangers of even this sort of thing can be minimized if there's a team of people responsible for creating the teaching content and then holding one another accountable for how it's delivered.

There is one more big issue that young people have to deal with when there is only one person or couple responsible for the youth ministry. If they have a concern about the leadership, they have no place to go to voice that concern. If they feel that the youth worker might be out of line in some way—or even just nearing a questionable line—there's no one to discuss that with to get another perspective. Students are much more comfortable, and the youth ministry is much healthier, when they have options and know that their concerns will be taken seriously.

THE OPPORTUNITY TO MODEL SKILLS OF COMMUNITY AND RELATIONSHIP

One of the most important benefits generated when we intentionally approach ministry with a team mentality is that we're given the opportunity to model for our students what healthy Christian community looks like. We serve a generation that listens with its eyes. These young people are watching carefully to learn all they can from the adults in their lives. Many of them don't have healthy role models who warrant watching.

As a youth ministry team we have the opportunity to show kids in a tangible, visible way what healthy, spiritual friendship looks like. Young men have the opportunity to observe older men and see how they treat each other and, of course, how they treat the women who are on the team. In the same way, young women have the privilege of observing older women in relationships. Beyond that, if there are married couples in leadership, teens will (hopefully) get the opportunity to see firsthand what a healthy marriage looks like. I can't count the number of students who, over the years, have told me that the marriage of their youth pastor, small group leader, or mentor was the one they had observed most closely as they shaped their own ideas of what a healthy marriage was all about.

A healthy team can demonstrate all sorts of basic relational skills for the students being led: how to participate effectively in a shared decision-making process, how to serve one another in love, and how to resolve conflict well should it arise.

TRUTH FROM THE TRENCHES

We serve a generation that listens with its eyes. These young people are watching carefully to learn all they can from the adults in their lives. Many of them don't have healthy role models who warrant watching.

This subtle benefit to students—modeling healthy, proper relationships—may be undervalued because of the subtle, silent nature of it. In some ways it's simply a by-product of what we do as a team to make the ministry run smoothly, but it's such an important by-product. Good ministry team members regularly ask themselves what they're communicating to those they lead without even realizing it.

THE SHEER JOY AND BLESSING OF IT

We were created for relationship. The Trinity of the Father, Son, and Holy Spirit exists in relationship, and from the very beginning of creation God has designed us to enjoy fellowship with one another. There are few joys in life that compare with being surrounded by a group of like-minded people that is working together to accomplish something significant. It's not at all unusual for people in a church or community to look at a well-led youth ministry team and wish they could be part of it. The spontaneous laughter, creative freedom, and endless memories such a group shares makes it the kind of ministry everyone wants to join. Doing youth ministry as part of a team is fun, and when you're part of a team that knows how to work and play together, it doesn't get any better.

The thoughts in the first section of this book form a basis to get our discussion started. We've talked about some of the reasons we might (wrongly) resist the idea of team ministry, and we've looked at some of the benefits that come when we do teams well. But we've still got a long way to go before we've put it all together or really made it work.

ACTION PLAN

★ Here's a fun way to put together leadership discussion groups of four people each. Take apart a small flashlight—battery, barrel, end cap, bulb—or several if you have lots of people on your team. Hand each person one part of the flashlight. (One trick to add to this game is to not give each group all four needed parts.) Turn out the lights and then challenge your leaders to find the other people who have the parts needed to complete the reassembly of the flashlight. Then have your groups use their flashlights to read 1 Corinthians 12:12-26 together. (Don't worry if there are some extra pieces left over in the end.) Ask:

- How does what we've just done here reflect the truth of 1 Corinthians 12?
- What's the indispensable piece of the flashlight? (Answer: each piece is needed.)
- Which part is less important? (Answer: it can't work if even one piece is missing.)
- How did those of you feel who didn't have enough pieces to complete your assignment?

THINKING THROUGH LONE RANGERS, TEAMS, AND TEAMWORK

★ How well does our leadership team model strong relationships and healthy principles of community? What could we do to strengthen the lessons we teach our students who watch us relating to one another as leaders?

★ Does our group accurately reflect the diversity in our community? What other areas of diversity do we need to become more intentional about developing on our team?

★ What are some ways that working as a team creates a safer environment for our students? What are some areas we could strengthen in terms of safety and accountability?

★ Who are some people in our church or community who might make strong additions to our team?

PART TWO

PUTTING IT TOGETHER

PUTTING TOGETHER A TEAM WITH SUBSTANCE

As youth ministry has evolved and grown up through the past forty to fifty years, the role of the ministry team member has changed considerably. In the early years volunteers were generally cast in the role of activity planner, chaperone, and Bible instructor. Of course, those were entirely appropriate roles when youth ministry consisted of large, activity-centered events and predictably structured times of religious education. But as we know, the world of youth ministry has changed dramatically. The best word to describe what has happened would be *decentralization*. While in the past the ministry energy was centered around a charismatic individual who did his ministry (the male pronoun here was chosen intentionally) from up front aided by a few assistants who served as chaperones and security guards, the most effective work with teenagers now is in low-ratio, intimate, relational clusters. This has created several notable outcomes.

First, the responsibility for youth ministry is now often spread much more broadly. To keep ministry ratios low, more people are needed in the lives of teenagers than ever before. And they are there to meet relational needs, not just to chaperone students through a few events. Also, this responsibility is now carried by a much more diverse group of people. Having lots of people involved is a wonderful blessing, but it also brings with it some significant new responsibilities in the areas of screening, training, supervision, nurture, and care.

Next, because of these low ratios, the levels of trust that develop in these ministry relationships intensify as well. Students will often share, and on a deep level, the secrets of their lives that previously would have been off limits to any adult. This makes it more important than ever to carefully train and equip volunteers for their roles. We're not just looking for someone who can pull off an event or communicate some biblical content. We're looking for someone who can be trusted to walk deeply into the life of a teenager. It's a very different job description than it used to be.

The responsibility to properly prepare our team members to handle the complexity of very transparent relationships is something that must be taken seriously. This issue will be addressed more thoroughly later in the book because it truly redefines the role of a team leader. But it's not just about the quality of leadership that a team gets. At a very basic level it's about the raw material of that team itself. The current paradigm of an intentionally relational youth ministry demands that we select team members of quality and maturity.

CHARACTER QUALITIES THAT SPELL "REAL EFFECTIVENESS"

"All we really need are people who love God and love kids!" Some have suggested that those two factors are enough to qualify someone for a position as a potential youth ministry team member. All of us would agree that those are pretty basic starting points, but we should realize that there's a lot more to it than that. The nature of youth ministry actually demands quite a bit more if we want to see young lives transformed.

As was suggested earlier in the book, with the lives of teenagers becoming more and more complicated, it becomes increasingly important to ensure that the adults we invite onto our ministry team are men and women of character.

So what are these character traits that increase the effectiveness of those who work with students? As I pondered this question I grabbed my journal and began to jot down the names of youth workers I've known through the years who have been unusually effective. It didn't take me long to come up with a list of more than fifty outstanding men and women—mostly volunteers—who made a significant impact in the lives of the teenagers they worked with.

As I reviewed my list I began to jot down the character qualities that described those individuals. I wasn't looking for external things like age, education, fashion sense, athletic ability, techno-savviness, the cool factor, or any of the other stereotypical things we often (inappropriately) associate with youth ministry suitability. As I thought about the deeper issues that defined these people, I was amazed to see how much they had in common. With only a few trips to the thesaurus I was able to summarize my observations with a list of seventeen personal qualities and character traits that spell REAL EFFECTIVENESS. I think they're worth considering in the people we invite onto our teams.

As you look through the list and my brief explanation of each descriptor (these unpack the term a bit more with the essential qualities, as I see them, of healthy youth workers) you might ask yourself how you and some of your coworkers would rate on a scale of one to ten. By the way, in case you hadn't noticed,

R	Relatively free of personal problems
E	Emotional Intelligence
A	Authenticity
L	Loving heart
E	Encouraging
F	Flexibility
F	Faithfulness
E	Examined life
C	Creativity
T	Teachable spirit
I	Integrity
V	Visionary
E	Enthusiastic
N	Natural leadership ability
E	Energetic
S	Servant-hearted
S	Sense of humor

the only person who scores straight tens on this is Jesus—and maybe the senior pastor of your church. (OK, that was a joke.) So don't go looking for perfection. Not in your life or in the lives of your volunteers.

R–Relatively free of personal problems

An absence of relational baggage, unresolved conflicts, and financial, psychological, or legal unfinished business

This is an important place to start. Obviously, none of us are completely baggage-free, but when that baggage defines an individual, or looms so large that it distracts them from functioning in a healthy way, he or she needs to be given the opportunity to get healthy before trying to help others. Unfortunately, a lot of this pent-up stuff expresses itself in relationally destructive ways when stress levels increase. When that happens, the person who was supposed to be positioned as a helper actually becomes an additional burden and creates an atmosphere that is counterproductive to what we're trying to accomplish in the lives of teens. As a general rule, we should never invite someone into a youth ministry role because "it will really be good for them" as they try to work through their junk.

TRUTH FROM THE TRENCHES

As a general rule, never invite someone into a youth ministry role because "it will really be good for them" as they try to work through the emotional baggage from their past.

E–Emotional intelligence

Consciously aware of one's own emotions, able to make choices regarding the expression of those emotions, and able to accurately discern one's emotional impact on others

A lot has been written recently in business and leadership circles about the phenomenon of emotional intelligence. All of us have seen examples of people who are emotionally dense. They stuff their negative emotions, often denying that they even exist. Then they vent those previously denied emotions randomly without any consideration as to how their outbursts may impact others. Often their emotional responses are completely out of sync and out of proportion with what is actually going on as they under- or overreact. Obviously, these folks won't do well with teenagers who desperately need models of emotional health as they ride their own roller coaster of adolescent affect.

A–Authenticity

The ability to relate to others with an appropriate level of chosen transparency, self-disclosure, and relational honesty

A commitment to living honestly is absolutely critical to an effective ministry with teens. They have enormous respect for people who choose to live this way and are able to sniff out an imposter from miles away. Phoniness, hypocrisy, and superficiality—some teens call the people who display these characteristics plastic, or posers—are the quickest ways to kill the trust of a young person. Because trust is at the heart of any meaningful ministry relationship, adults who work with teens must intentionally cultivate character qualities that will open relational doors. This component of character is so central that we'll give it more attention on its own a bit later on.

TRUTH FROM THE TRENCHES

Teenagers have an enormous respect for people who choose to live honestly and openly, who display authenticity in their lives. Teens are able to sniff out an imposter from miles away.

L–Loving heart

A willingness to put the personal and spiritual growth of another person ahead of the natural commitment to one's own safety and comfort

The problem with talking about love is that it has become so clichéd it hardly means anything anymore. The truth is that when youth workers are truly committed to loving students according to the biblical definition and example of Christ, it's one of the riskiest things they can do. To willingly sacrifice my own safety so another person can benefit is the ultimate act of human love. Unfortunately the 1 Corinthians 13 description of love has been applied mostly at weddings, but if we were to evaluate the quality of our communities by that standard, I'm afraid some of us would be found wanting.

E–Encouraging

Able to sense the fear and apprehension in others and respond by infusing courage through empowering words and caring presence

Adolescence is a challenging time for even the most confident of the students we work with. The anxieties and concerns that are part of the everyday life of a teenager are often hidden behind a thin facade of bravado that is meant to keep most adults at a distance. A good youth worker will be able to get inside the walls that teenagers hide behind and respond at a deep and meaningful level to fears and uncertainties by speaking words of truth and courage. We can simply never give too much encouragement to a teenager.

TRUTH FROM THE TRENCHES

A youth leader can simply never give too much encouragement to a teenager.

F–Flexibility

Light on one's feet; open and able to adapt to short-notice changes; not rigid and predictable

It doesn't matter how carefully the plans are laid or how meticulously the details have been checked and double-checked, youth ministry is always full of surprises. The bus breaks down. The bulb burns out. The rainstorm blows in. The guest speaker gets caught in traffic. The amazing game you found online turns out to be a bust with your kids. Six show up when you had planned for sixty, or vice versa. A carful of kids are in a serious accident on Saturday night and suddenly that Sunday morning study on Levitical sacrifice doesn't seem very relevant. Good youth workers roll with the punches. The ability to make adjustments quickly when circumstances change is an absolute necessity.

TRUTH FROM THE TRENCHES

Good youth workers roll with the punches. The ability to make adjustments quickly when circumstances change is an absolute necessity.

F–Faithfulness

Always trustworthy; no excuses; the job is done right

Living a life of ministry faithfulness is not only a gift to the students we serve and to our fellow team members, it's actually an act of worship and obedience. A faithful team member can be counted on to be there, take responsibility, follow through, and finish well. Good team play depends on individuals who are committed to faithfulness. In the absence of faithfulness, leaders are left with no choice but to double-check, create contingency plans, and do things themselves instead of trusting that they will be done well by the person they were delegated to. Of course, it goes without saying that faithfulness to God, to one's spouse and family, and to the mission of your organization is job one.

E–Examined life

An accurate view of both strengths and weaknesses based on a courageous commitment to being brutally honest with oneself

The psalmist David prayed a bold prayer when he said, "Search me, O God, and know my heart" (Psalm 139:23). What he was acknowledging was that he (as is the case with each of us) lived with certain blind spots that he was incapable of seeing unless God were to open his eyes. This kind of intentionality is necessary for anyone who wants to have an effective ministry in the life of a teenager. Self-monitoring is hard and often painful work and can uncover truth that we'd rather not see, but in order for us to function well on a ministry team we must be deeply aware of our strengths, weaknesses, vulnerabilities, gifts, abilities, addictions, and anything else that defines us.

> Search me, O God, and know my heart; test me and know my anxious thoughts.
> See if there is any offensive way in me, and lead me in the way everlasting.
>
> PSALM 139:23, 24

Socrates said, "The unexamined life is not worth living." I would suggest that an unexamined life is not worth sharing. If we believe that our lives are our most significant instruments of ministry, we should be committed to intentionally sharpening those lives through regularly looking deeply into the mirrors of our souls, embracing what we find, and choosing to live honestly in light of that knowledge.

C–Creativity

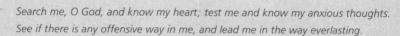

Able to dream and envision—to see things as they could be instead of how they are; willing to try something without knowing the outcome ahead of time

I am astounded at the number of people who declare with confidence that they are simply not creative. If we believe that we are made in the image of God, we must accept that creativity is woven into our very nature. I'm not suggesting that creativity comes naturally, because the nature of God in us has been messed up by the fear that entered our lives with our sinfulness.

What I am saying is that each of us was born with an innate desire to create, to envision, and to imagine things as they could be.

Sadly, most of us confront a wall of fear long before that creativity ever has an opportunity to be expressed. Children imagine, play, dance, sing, paint, and draw—expressing without inhibition the creativity that God has placed in each of them. By the time they reach their adolescence much of that creativity has been stifled, and by the time they are adults it will be virtually invisible in all but a few. Good youth workers are an exception. They still have that mischievous twinkle in their eye and willingness to try something without knowing how it will turn out. When teens see adults who embrace their creativity, it gives them courage to explore their own—and in the process sets them up for a much freer, healthier adulthood.

T–Teachable spirit

A humble willingness to listen and learn from others; not always having to be right

One of the toughest character qualities for us to cultivate is a truly teachable spirit. Deep inside most of us there is an arrogant assumption that we have it all figured out. Good youth workers, by contrast, realize that there is a great deal to be learned from the students we rub shoulders with each day and from our fellow team members. One of the biggest mistakes I made in my early years of volunteer youth ministry was to assume that the delivery of truth was a one-way process. I was the one who had prepared. I was the one who had the background to discern what was right and what was wrong. So the job of my students was to sit passively and listen while I poured out my pearls of wisdom on them. It was only when I began to recognize that God could speak great truth into the heart of a teenager that I began to benefit as I learned to listen to their insights and observations. A commitment to being a lifelong learner—wherever that learning comes from—is the path to a truly enriched life of ministry.

I–Integrity

Lives an intentionally principled life; what is seen on the outside is an accurate reflection of what exists on the inside

The news these days seems to be filled with stories of highly visible leaders who sacrifice their integrity for some form of selfish gain. Whether it's a politician or a pastor, a business leader or a professional athlete, there are plenty of examples of what a lack of integrity leads to. The essence of integrity is a commitment to being the same person no matter what the context is. As a youth worker that means the person the students see leading the Bible study on Tuesday night is the same person they would see in the workplace, at the gym, or at a party with friends on a Friday night. Because a person of integrity is shaped by principles, there is a welcome consistency in their identity no matter what the circumstances. We often underestimate how important it is for teenagers to see this kind of integrity modeled. Because they're in the midst of establishing their own personal identity, and thinking through the values and beliefs on which they will build their lives, a role model of integrity will help them learn how to live that way.

V–Visionary

Capable of seeing the big picture—able to identify the potential in a person or in a situation when others may not see a thing

The ability to see in a young person what most people don't is one key aptitude that can set an effective youth worker apart from others. Teenagers too often have been cast in a negative light. Even within the church the needs of adolescents are often not well understood. Young people usually respond positively when they know they're in a relationship with someone who sees the best in them. Leaders who have this kind of vision don't keep their observations to themselves. They become advocates to the rest of the community, speaking positively about the teenagers they know whenever they have the opportunity. They speak affirming truth into the lives of the teens they work with and in the process generate something for a young person to aspire to. Not only do they see the potential in students, they also see opportunities for ministry that others may miss. All of this comes as a result of viewing the world through God's eyes. His vision is always bigger than anything we can generate at a human level.

E–Enthusiastic

Contagiously optimistic and full of life; a life that overflows

Enthusiasm does not need to be loud and boisterous to be contagious, but the passion of an effective youth worker must be evident. Most of us who work with teenagers have firsthand experience with the apathy that seems to mark this generation. Stirring up a passion in today's teens for nearly anything sometimes feels like an impossible task. A lifeless youth worker will simply reinforce the indifference that kids often bring to the youth group. I'm not suggesting that we churn up a false enthusiasm, but instead that we cultivate a genuine passion for what it is we do—whether we're diving into a Bible study or giving our full enthusiasm to an activity we're leading. We want our students to cultivate a life that overflows with the joy that comes from living in Christ's presence. For that to happen our own joy must be evident.

TRUTH FROM THE TRENCHES

Enthusiasm does not need to be loud and boisterous to be contagious. But the passion of a youth worker must be evident.

N–Natural leadership ability

Able to inspire people to work together to accomplish a task

Leadership ability is not something that can be fully learned, in my opinion, but instead is something given naturally by God. However, it can be sharpened when it is already present. What is this leadership thing? It's a mysterious combination of temperament, character, motivation, experience, giftedness, and passion that inspires other people to follow. This is not to say that leadership skills can't be taught. In fact, we should make every effort to sharpen the leadership skills and abilities that both our adult and student leaders possess. The knack for being a leader, however, is something quite different, and when we find someone who has this ability we need to position them in ministry to make the most of it. Natural leaders get things done, but never by themselves. They have the unique ability to rally others to a cause and to share the excitement of a job completed with all those who have participated. Young people are looking for leaders they can follow.

E–Energetic

Possessing vigor, strength, and endurance; the willingness and ability to persevere

Even the most low-key youth worker who is effective with teenagers has an inner vigor and strength that is unmistakable. Youth ministry can be exhausting. The relational load, the late nights, the physical demands of camping trips, missions projects, fund-raisers, and even the crazy games we play require a level of energy that not everyone has. The fact is, working with kids will require an above average energy level and people whose life demands leave them with no energy to spare will likely not have much to contribute in youth ministry. There is one significant piece of good news in all this—simply being around teenagers we love can create energy.

S–Servant-hearted

More concerned with God's "well done" than with the applause of people

Among the most compelling pictures of the character of Christ are those where his humility is most evident. That evening in the upper room as he knelt in front of each of his disciples to wash their dusty feet he was communicating the very heart of what it would mean to represent him to the world. It is not a natural or common thing for an adult to enter the world of a teenager for the purpose of serving them in Jesus' name. But it is a powerful reflection of what he demonstrated when he chose to leave behind the privileges of being God to enter our world so that the glory of God would be clearly visible (John 1:14; Philippians 2:5-7). It is important for us to understand that there is a big difference between catering to a demanding generation and serving it in humility and love. Youth ministry can be a thankless job and for those who need constant affirmation it may be disappointing. But for those who understand Paul's exhortation that "your attitude should be the same as that of Christ Jesus" (Philippians 2:5), there is great reward in choosing a servant attitude as we minister to teenagers.

Your attitude should be the same as that of Christ Jesus:
Who, being in very nature God, did not consider equality with God something to be grasped,
but made himself nothing, taking the very nature of a servant, being made in human likeness.

PHILIPPIANS 2:5-7

S–Sense of humor

Laughs easily; doesn't take oneself too seriously; is able to give and take a joke

What a great place for our list to end. Youth workers without a sense of humor just don't last long. Lighten up! Teenagers need adults in their lives who show them how to have a good time. One of the great gifts that a youth worker gives the students in his or her care is to model what appropriate humor looks like and where to draw the line. Show your students that there are lots of things in this world that are genuinely funny but also teach them to discern when humor becomes inappropriate and destructive. There is plenty of room in youth ministry for practical jokes, pranks, and fun. We all understand that the stakes are high and that discipling teenagers is serious business. But a healthy dose of laughter modeled by an adult leader is a great way to set the tone for deeper trust and more meaningful relationships.

TRUTH FROM THE TRENCHES

One of the great gifts a youth worker gives the students in his or her care is to model what appropriate humor looks like and where to draw the line.

ACTION PLAN

★ Which three of the character traits listed in this chapter are your strongest? Which three represent the biggest challenges for you personally? Pick one of the three that is a challenge and develop a plan for strengthening that area of your life.

PUTTING TOGETHER
A VOLUNTEER TEAM
STUDENTS WILL LOVE

ou don't have to work with them for too long before you realize what really matters to a teenager. As most of us know, every teenager needs a caring, nonparental adult speaking into their lives to guide and accompany them as they navigate the challenges of adolescence. We've taken the time to explore the kind of character qualities that will suit a person well for working with kids, but from a teenager's perspective it's generally much simpler than that. When it gets right down to it, what kids are looking for is an adult who is simply available, accepting, and authentic. The only problem, however, is that each of these three factors can become destructive, even toxic, when they're offered without careful consideration of appropriate boundaries.

AVAILABLE

It doesn't get any more basic than this in youth ministry. If you're not able to be available, it really doesn't matter how accepting or authentic you might be. A teenager might make a few attempts to connect, but if the message they receive is that you don't have the time or the relational energy to invest, they will generally not try to push their way into a friendship. Adolescents are able to sense almost immediately whether an offer of relationship is genuine. If it feels like an adult is serving out of duty or obligation, teenagers will keep their distance. They have plenty of obliged adults in their lives already. What they're looking for is an adult who genuinely wants to be there. Being available means that you not only have space in your personal calendar for them but also that you have room in your heart. This is why it's so important to keep our ministry ratios low and our teams as diverse as possible.

But wait a minute! What happens when a youth worker offers a student availability without any boundaries? "Hey, I just want you to know that I'm available for you 24/7. I know there have been plenty of people in your life who have told you they were available and then when you needed them they just weren't there. I'm not going to be another one of those people. You can count on me. Call me anytime. I will always be there for you." Does that sound familiar? Unfortunately, there are plenty of well-meaning youth workers who think that being available means just that.

TRUTH FROM THE TRENCHES

If it feels like an adult is serving out of duty or obligation, teenagers will keep their distance. They have plenty of obliged adults in their lives already.

There are more than a few problems with offering students that level of availability. The first problem is that it's simply a lie. As much as we'd love to be endlessly available, there will be exceptions. At some point you'll need to get into the shower, or you'll be on an airplane, or at your aunt Bertha's funeral. And when one of those exceptions is experienced it will represent another betrayal for a teenager who has very likely felt abandoned before. In addition, teens are smart enough to know that no one can always be available, and when we promise that we will be, they'll become suspicious of our integrity.

But let's just assume for a moment that it might be possible to provide a student with 24/7 availability. Think about the unhealthy and distorted relational dynamics this sets up between an adult and a young person. A technical term that might describe this sort of an arrangement is *codependence*. In its simplest terms it means that two people have an unspoken—and often unacknowledged—commitment to allowing each other to remain unhealthy in their relationship. Basically, an adult is saying, "I'll let you lean on me in some really unhealthy ways as long as you let me need to be needed in some equally unhealthy ways." Ultimately, a pattern like this will do great damage to the primary relationships of a volunteer youth worker. Marriages will suffer and families will be shortchanged, perhaps even becoming resentful towards the overscheduled team member. Adult friendships will begin to disappear because of the constant priority given to student ministry. All these things can lead to a very imbalanced life for the well-meaning person. Before long youth workers become overwhelmed with the constant barrage of late night emergency calls and increasingly frantic demands, and the only option left is to walk away from ministry completely. Burned out and defeated, they become another casualty of their good intentions.

But perhaps the biggest problem with availability without boundaries is that it reinforces a dangerous notion—for both the youth worker and the adolescent. The youth worker develops a bit of a messiah complex, sincerely believing that the Trinity is looking for a fourth member and convinced that they are that one. But even more happens: at the same time, the student gets the idea that God is a "Plan B" strategy for dealing with pain, hardship, questions, and struggles and is to be invoked only when all human options have been exhausted. Obviously, this combination of factors pushes the presence of Christ to the sidelines of a ministry and robs it of all the potential transformational power he could bring to the lives of students and leaders alike if he were given his rightful place.

I need to constantly remind myself of Paul's words when he said, "Brothers, think of what you were when you were called. Not many of you were wise by human standards; not many were influential; not many were of noble birth. But God chose the foolish things of the world to shame the wise; God chose the weak things of the world to shame the strong. He chose the lowly things of this world and the despised things . . . so that no one may boast before him" (1 Corinthians 1:26-29). What Paul is saying is that when good things happen in the lives of students, it's because God has done something, not because of our own wisdom, influence, or strength. There is no room for boasting. He gets the glory.

ACCEPTING

Students are looking for adults who are willing to love them as they are. Unconditional acceptance is not something they get a lot of—especially from the adults around them. Even well-meaning parents often communicate in subtle (and not so subtle) ways that it's performance, achievement, and success that earn their kids affirmation and affection. Our whole culture reinforces the notion that unless someone is wearing the right brands, carrying the right technology, living in the right part of town, going to the right school, shaped like a supermodel with a clear complexion and a pretty face to match . . . they are unaccepted. Teenagers who feel unaccepted in multiple relational environments quickly begin to feel that they *are* unacceptable; the difference between those two worlds is immense. When their assessment begins to touch their very sense of identity, it takes a deep toll. They often conclude that the reason they are not being accepted is because there is something inherently defective about them. This leaves them only a few options. They can camouflage their perceived areas of defectiveness and hope that no one notices—this feels like massive pressure to most teenagers. Another option is to overcompensate in the areas where they feel they are lacking—often leading to teens feeling driven and obsessed with presenting a front they know is not truthful. Or they can simply resign themselves to the fact that they are unworthy of relationships and withdraw into a lonely, often angry world of isolation.

Finding adults for your ministry team who are truly accepting of teenagers with all their behavioral quirks, developmental ups and downs, and relational inconsistencies is quite a challenge. But when teens know they are accepted as they are, they can relax, participate, and enjoy the safety of belonging. A fundamental rule of youth ministry is that teenagers will generally not be spiritually responsive until they feel socially accepted. Building a team of adults who love teens as they are must be a priority.

TRUTH FROM THE TRENCHES

Teens will generally not be spiritually responsive until they feel socially accepted. We must build teams of adults who love teens as they are.

But wait a minute! What happens when a youth worker offers a student acceptance without any standards? "Hey—don't worry about me. You don't need to make any changes for our relationship to work. I know there are lots of adults who would judge you for your language, the substances you use and abuse, your attitude, your sexual choices . . . But you won't find me ragging on you for that stuff. I accept you as you are." Obviously, the danger of offering acceptance without limits is that students never get appropriately challenged to move beyond where they are, toward where they could be. An imbalance toward cheap grace gives students license to continue to live as they please and negates the value of a spiritually mature adult in their life. It's a fine line we walk when we look for ways to show students that we accept them even though we may not accept some of their choices.

What we're talking about here is the appropriate place of grace in youth ministry relationships. Grace recognizes that teenagers are people in transition who need plenty of support, encouragement, and second chances, and if we are going to err with teenagers we should likely err on the side of grace. But having said that, we must recognize that failing to hold students accountable for growth is a compromise of our ministry purpose at the most fundamental level.

The secret is to find ways to assure students through both our words and our actions that our love for them is not conditional, while calling them to become the best they can possibly be. In fact, when we fail to hold kids to a high standard of growth and development, we are actually abdicating our role in their lives. The reason a youth worker gets tangled up in the story of a teenager in the first place is to call them to become more like Jesus—wherever they happen to be on their journey.

When we communicate acceptance with no standards, several outcomes can be anticipated. The first is that young people will quickly lose respect for us. They know that a spiritually mature adult represents a standard that is higher than one with no boundaries. They want and expect us to challenge them in the areas that need growth. That combination of true and deep affection coupled with the expectation of transformation is something most teens don't get very much of. Movies like *Coach Carter, Mr. Holland's Opus, Freedom Writers, Mad Hot Ballroom,* and dozens of others we've seen celebrate the power of adults who have found that balance in the lives of the teenagers. It's tough love and most of the kids I've known long for it.

Another outcome of unprincipled acceptance is youth ministry chaos. Pushing boundaries seems to be written into the job description of most teenagers. They will try to get away with as much as they can. A leader who loves blindly is often seen as weak, and when students confront weakness they push hard. I've spoken to plenty of adult youth workers who are frustrated because of the bedlam they confront every time their youth group meets. In many cases it was simply an absence of expectations. Unfortunately, a lot of the students we work with today come from family situations where standards have been low and a great deal of freedom has been given. These things can make it tough to set standards at first, but in the end the rewards will be well worth it.

TRUTH FROM THE TRENCHES

A leader who loves blindly is often seen as weak, and when students confront weakness they push hard. When there is bedlam in a youth group—or an individual life—it's often simply the outcome of an absence of expectations.

Of course there is a theological concern that also must be acknowledged. When we model a relationship that is all affection with no expectations, it's easy for our students to develop a very distorted view of God as well. They begin to view him as weak. He becomes a sweet old grandpa who just wants to make their lives happy. It's easy to pull the wool over his eyes and get away with anything. Jesus loved his disciples deeply. That was obvious. But he also called them to a higher standard of holiness. The same could be said of the apostle

Paul in his deep love for the churches he planted and then corresponded with. His affection for them was unmistakable, but he was constantly challenging them to become all that they were meant to be.

Here's the bottom line: we love our students as they are but we refuse to leave them as they are. And if we don't do it, chances are no one else will.

AUTHENTIC

Kids can smell a phony from a mile away. They long for relationships that are honest, transparent, and trustworthy both with their peers and with the adults they know. In fact, most students would tell you that without that kind of openness there can be no trust. The candidness that marks the relationships that teens have with each other blows me away. They talk freely about almost anything—especially when they are interacting online. Their lives seem to be open books to one another. Adults who hide behind masks will rarely get invited into these deeper places where teenagers connect.

Teens routinely express disdain for adults who pretend that everything is fine when clearly it's not. They see the hypocrisy that often exists in shallow relationships that are politically correct but lack substance. As a generation they have determined that they will not live that way. If we want to connect deeply with the students in our care, we must choose to live authentically with them. There is no room for pretense, dishonesty, posturing, and pretending. When they struggle they find great hope in the fact that we struggle too. When they doubt it encourages them to know that we have our doubts as well. When they face failure they will find little comfort in an adult who pretends that nothing has ever gone wrong.

TRUTH FROM THE TRENCHES

If we want to connect deeply with the students in our care, we must choose to live authentically with them. There is no room for pretense, dishonesty, posturing, and pretending.

Paul reinforces this notion in 1 Thessalonians 2:8 when he says, "We loved you so much that we were delighted to share with you not only the gospel of God but our lives as well, because you had become so dear to us." The reality of youth ministry is that our kids will see us as we are. Because it's about doing life together, there isn't a lot of room to hide. They see us at our best and our worst. Your most significant instrument of ministry is your life, lived visibly, openly, and transparently before a young generation so that they can see the difference the gospel of Jesus makes in you.

But wait a minute. What happens when we offer our students uncensored authenticity? Do they really need to know every doubt and every deep, dark secret in our lives for us to have an impact?

★ "Hey, I just want to be totally honest with you guys. Frankly, I'm not buying much of this Christianity stuff these days. The whole thing just seems like one big made-up story. Just sharing that with you so you know where I'm at right now."

★ "My marriage just feels like it's been in the Dumpster lately. We're fighting all the time and our sex life has never been worse."

★ "Guys, I have not been able to stay off those porn sites. Just want to be totally honest with you so you know what's happening for me these days."

Does any of that feel like it crosses a line? Of course. Obviously, there are limits to how transparent an adult ought to be with a young person.

PRINCIPLES TO LEAD BY

Perhaps a few principles would be in order. The first has to do with age appropriateness. Because youth ministry relationships are by definition intergenerational, we must constantly monitor what levels of communication are allowed to cross the bridge from adult to teenager. If the issues we're facing in our lives are not commonly part of the life of a teenager, there is likely very little value they will gain from hearing about them. That's not to say that these adult issues should not be shared at all. In fact, this is where healthy, mutual, supportive relationships with other adults are so important for the people on our teams.

A second principle has to do with what is motivating our desire to share transparently. There are so many illegitimate motivations available to us. Sometimes it's just about getting it off our chest—the word is catharsis. We need someone to vent to, and since we are spending most of our time with teenagers, they find themselves in the line of fire. Sometimes inappropriate sharing is motivated by a desire for quick bonding. We desperately want to be accepted and we believe that any self-disclosure will accomplish that. There are times we expose deep things to get sympathy or to lower people's expectations or even to push people away. There is a huge difference between ministry-motivated transparency and emotional exhibitionism.

TRUTH FROM THE TRENCHES

Sometimes inappropriate sharing is motivated by a desire for quick bonding. We desperately want to be accepted and we believe that any self-disclosure will accomplish that.

Ephesians 4:29 gives us a helpful filter through which we can determine if our transparency is appropriate or not. We're told to say nothing that is unwholesome and to only say what will encourage, or build up, others. In this passage, Paul identifies three simple questions we must ask:

* ★ "Will this help to build up the teenager I share it with?" Some of what adults share with teenagers in the name of authenticity can be highly destructive.
* ★ "Is it based on their needs or mine?" Any sharing that is driven by my need to be heard rather than the needs of the young listener is out of line.
* ★ "Will the listener be benefited in any way for having heard my disclosure?" It's always good to consider exactly how we hope our transparent confessions will benefit those who listen.

Do not let any unwholesome talk come out of your mouths, but only what is helpful for building others up according to their needs, that it may benefit those who listen.

EPHESIANS 4:29

WRAPPING IT UP BEFORE WE MAKE IT WORK

Putting together a good team demands careful intentionality. The roles in which we cast the men and women who will serve students as small group leaders, mentors, coaches, Sunday school teachers, mission trip leaders, bus drivers, tutors, spiritual directors, and more, are primarily relational. This means that the raw material of who is chosen will be the primary determining factor in the overall quality of the team. In this section we talked about choosing men and women of character. Although the character qualities listed in chapter 4 may not respond specifically to consciously felt needs in the lives of our students, they will largely determine the ministry effectiveness of individual team members. In this chapter we've talked about men and women who connect with students deeply at the level of their consciously felt needs—the desire for adults who are available, accepting, and authentic. The danger, of course, is to recruit team members who don't understand what appropriateness in each of these areas looks like.

As we move into the third and most practical section of this book we'll explore specific ways to recruit, screen, train, and nurture our teams in a way that will position them for the greatest possible effectiveness in the lives of students.

ACTION PLAN

★ Why are healthy boundaries important? Think about where you've seen them produce fruit; think about where you've seen the crossing of healthy boundary lines cause trouble.

PUTTING TOGETHER AN EFFECTIVE TEAM

★ Look again at the characteristics of effective leadership; identify a student leader or two who embody many of these qualities. How could you make better use of the young leaders in your group?

★ Does the fact that you are a role model to teenagers justify an expectation for a higher standard of behavior in areas like media consumption, humor and language, alcohol use, the party scene, dating standards, and more? Support your position with Scripture.

★ How will you deal with a student who has unrealistic expectations of your availability and is becoming overwhelmingly demanding? What's a healthy plan to guard yourself without nullifying what the student is feeling?

★ How can you help each other maintain appropriate levels of availability, acceptance, and authenticity? What level of accountability in these areas are you willing to accept from other team members?

PART THREE

MAKING IT WORK

MAKING IT WORK BY
STARTING RIGHT

Well, here's where the proverbial Firestones meet the freeway. It's time to make it happen. We've thought about why teams matter and we've put together a picture of the kind of individuals we want on our teams. Now it's time to talk about how to get those people on the team, how to keep them there, and even how to get rid of them if it's not working out for some good reason.

By now it should be clear that not just anyone will do when it comes to building a solid youth ministry team. The stakes are high and the responsibility that comes with spiritually nurturing a generation of young lives is not to be taken lightly. This means that the recruitment process must be carried out strategically. The principles we'll explore and the process that is described can be applied in any ministry setting—church or parachurch, rural or urban, big or small.

HOW MANY?

The first step in the process is to assess the needs of the group and determine how large a team will be required to meet those needs. Most youth ministries I've observed are understaffed; this creates undue work and extra stress for the volunteers who have committed to the task. This in turn causes extra pressure, demands, and even guilt for the leader. An understaffed team operates in survival mode. Only the most urgent ministry needs are addressed and there is often little emotional energy left to dream about what could be done. In short, you can't have too many volunteers.

It goes without saying that the most effective ratio for youth ministry (or any kind of relational ministry for that matter) is one-to-one. Wouldn't it be a wonderful thing if each of the students in our care had a concerned adult who was committed to praying for them, supporting and encouraging them in their spiritual journey, and calling them to become all that God created them to be? It's not an impossible dream. A mentoring program—even for our students in their graduating year (maybe *especially* for students in their graduating year, considering the world they're about to step into)—might be a wonderful supplement to our weekly youth ministry programs. These mentors wouldn't be required to attend the weekly events, come on retreats, or lead small groups. They would function in addition to the regular youth ministry team and would provide a further level of care and nurture for each young person.

TRUTH FROM THE TRENCHES

An understaffed team operates in survival mode. Only the most urgent ministry needs are addressed and there is often little emotional energy left to dream about what could be done.

In youth ministry we've often talked about aiming for a ratio of one volunteer leader for every five students as an ideal goal for our basic leadership team. But Chap Clark, author, professor, and senior editor of Y*outh Worker Journal,* challenges us to think about ministry ratios in a whole new way. In a recent conversation Chap and I had, he suggested that we turn the 5:1 ratio upside down. We know that teenagers actually benefit immensely from multiple adult voices in their lives. Chap proposed that we ought to challenge faith communities to create an environment in which every young person has at least five adults who care about them, know their name, pray for them, notice if they were absent from church events, and provide an intergenerational connecting point to the faith family. It's a provocative and different way of thinking about the responsibility that a church has to embrace its young people and welcome them into community at the deepest levels.

For most of us, however, the responsibility of simply putting together a team to lead our small groups, staff our social events, and care for the basic ministry needs that our students represent is challenge enough. At this level, I would suggest that for junior high students a ratio of one adult for every four or five students is a reasonable goal and that for senior high students we would do well to provide one adult for every five to six students.

What, then, are some of the essential principles that must be kept in mind as our volunteer teams are assembled?

RECRUIT IN ANTICIPATION OF GROWTH

A reasonable mathematician might assume that a youth group of twenty students who are working with a ratio of 1:5 would need a team of four volunteers to accomplish its relational purposes. Easy stuff, right? At first glance we might agree that this takes care of the needs of a group of that size. However, there's a problem with this assumption. When four adults are caring for twenty students, each of them is already managing his or her maximum relational load. If the group should grow, someone on the volunteer team will immediately be working beyond his or her capacity. I would suggest that for a group of twenty students a team of five or six adults would create appropriate room for growth. To wait until the volunteers are overburdened creates unnecessary stress for everyone and actually makes it less attractive for students to bring their friends.

It takes faith to recruit in anticipation of growth, but most leaders who have been intentional about this strategy have found that it pays significant dividends.

NO CLONES ALLOWED

Even in a relatively small youth ministry there is great value in intentionally seeking diversity as you build your team of volunteers. Generally speaking, the diversity you're able to create on your adult team will be reflected in the kind of diversity you'll see in the students who are attracted to your group. Similar adults will attract a homogeneous and predictable group of similar kids. If you want your ministry to reflect the diversity that's found in the community of adolescents you serve, the first step is to ensure that your adult volunteers represent that same cross section of diversity.

When we speak of diversity the challenge is to consider this goal on a number of levels. Obviously, we must ensure gender diversity. A balanced mix of men and women is crucial to caring for both genders of teens. We must also recognize the importance of age diversity. The assumption that the ideal youth worker is an athletic, college-age student with an outgoing personality is a myth that must be dispelled. Teens need to have access to adults across the age spectrum. Both the wisdom of those who are older and the energetic zaniness of those who are younger have great value. And don't assume that some of the older folks can't be energetic and zany as well. I recently had the privilege of attending the twentieth anniversary of a youth ministry volunteer who had joined the youth staff in her sixties. Now an eightysomething, she is still full of life and vigor. The students absolutely adore her and were eager to hold this party to affirm the huge contribution she's made in their lives.

It's also good to have diverse personalities and temperaments on the team. Some students respond well to the loud, confident, sanguine personalities that seem to be naturally attracted to youth ministry, but others find these party animals to be intimidating and difficult to approach. They need people who are more thoughtful—perhaps even melancholic in their relational style. And don't overlook the fact that every good youth ministry team needs someone who is naturally analytical and loves to take care of details. This mix of personalities not only ensures that each student has a comfortable relational connecting point, but also that the wide range of tasks that need to be done is met by leaders whose temperaments naturally match the varying jobs.

We can't overlook the importance of putting together a team with diverse spiritual gifts. Because the work we are involved in is spiritual work, it's appropriate to seek a team with a balanced blend of spiritual gifts. Those who teach well, are hospitable, lead with confidence, have exceptional faith, or are gently merciful, to name but a few, together combine to create a spiritual strength that can move a group of young people forward in miraculous ways. It's amazing to see how often God will do his part to make sure that this mix of gifts will be perfectly suited to accomplish his purposes.

As I wrote in chapter 3, one of the great myths of life in community is the notion that each of us should strive to be "balanced." God created each of us to be imbalanced, eccentric, and marvelously unique. He seems to take great delight in using groups to create a divine equilibrium as each person lives out their uniqueness in an obedient way. That's what the body metaphor in 1 Corinthians chapter 12 is all about.

TRUTH FROM THE TRENCHES

Team members with a wide range of diverse gifts combine to create a spiritual strength that can move a group of young people forward in miraculous ways.

Ethnic diversity is an area in which many churches don't do well in. Although we serve in wonderfully colorful communities, our churches—and by extension our youth groups—are often starkly monotone. The richness that comes to a youth group that intentionally invites ethnic and cultural diversity is a benefit that too few ministries enjoy. The best way to communicate to students that ethnic diversity is valued is to offer a team of adult volunteers that is as colorful as the students you hope to attract.

TRUTH FROM THE TRENCHES

The best way to communicate to students that ethnic diversity is valued is to offer a team of adult volunteers that is as colorful as the students you hope to attract.

ACTION PLAN

★ Is it possible to implement Chap Clark's idea of five adults who know and care about each young person in your group? What are the first steps you'd need to take to move in that direction?

MAKING IT WORK: DIFFERENT FOLKS, DIFFERENT STROKES

In the early years of youth ministry it was assumed that when an individual joined the team they were making a costly commitment to a consuming ministry role. It was generally expected that a team member would attend all, or most, of the youth ministry activities and events. This often involved a Sunday morning teaching assignment, a weeknight Bible study, a weekend social activity, several out-of-town retreats, the fund-raisers that made those retreats affordable, a missions trip or two each year, and a few parent meetings to round out the package. In addition, the team member would be expected to attend volleyball games, piano recitals, and the drama that one of their small group students had a nonspeaking part in . . . and, of course, to be available for those midnight phone calls, hospital visits, and Coke dates that would ensure a growing relationship with students. (Just writing those last two sentences tired me out!) And even all that doesn't cover the planning meetings and training events that a good leader would expect his team to be part of. It's no wonder a lot of really gifted people cringe at the thought of becoming a youth ministry volunteer.

The truth is that you will still find the occasional volunteer who's willing to jump into the deep end and be involved in almost every aspect of the ministry you provide for your students. But it's important to recognize that not everyone can commit at that level, nor should they be expected to. The secret to broad involvement is to find places in which people with various levels of time and energy commitment can serve. Let's explore some of these options.

TRUTH FROM THE TRENCHES

You'll find the occasional volunteer who's willing to jump into the deep end and be involved in almost every aspect of ministry. But it's important to recognize that not everyone can commit at that level, nor should they be expected to. The secret is broad involvement.

PRAYER TEAM

Consider offering people the opportunity to be involved at the level of being a prayer partner. This is a role that almost anyone in your faith community can engage in. It's a wonderful way to involve senior citizens or others who might not feel comfortable in a face-to-face relationship with a teenager, or for busy people who just aren't available to be involved on a weekly basis. They can be partnered with a teenager with whom they would make a good match, or you can give them a short list of names of students in a small group and ask them to pray for those students. You can ask them to pray for various groups: the leadership team, a missions trip team, the worship band, new believers, or the student leaders. And it's a great idea to provide an opportunity for prayer partners and the youth group to get together for a face-to-face celebration of their relationship, perhaps once a year or even more often. Just don't treat this group as peripheral or insignificant. If in fact we believe in the power of prayer, these may turn out to be among the most important members of our team.

TRUTH FROM THE TRENCHES

Offer people the opportunity to be involved at the level of being a prayer partner. This is a role that almost anyone in your faith community can engage in. It's a wonderful way to engage people on a simple but meaningful level.

MENTORS

The next level of commitment should involve people who are willing to mentor a young person. There is no expectation that these adults attend any of the regular weekly meetings, activities, or events on the youth ministry calendar. Instead, they find a way within their schedule to get together one-on-one with some predefined regularity—once a week if possible or as little as once a month—for the purpose of guiding a young person toward spiritual maturity through an ongoing intentional ministry relationship. Not every student is ready for this kind of a spiritual relationship, so it might be best to offer it as an option for those who desire this level of input. Then trust God to provide a good match for each of the students who expresses an interest.

MINISTRY SPECIALISTS

Another category of volunteer that does not require regular weekly participation in scheduled activities is that of the ministry specialist who is invited to participate on an occasional basis to address a specific short-term need that might arise in the youth group. Like the designated hitter on a baseball team, this individual steps in to bring what they do best—often as a one-time (or only a handful of times) investment. This role could include a team of cooks for a retreat weekend, a first-aid specialist, an emergency medical technician, a medical doctor who comes along on a wilderness adventure, a carpenter to help a team of students build a drama set, a language instructor to prepare a missions team for an overseas trip, a bus driver, a boat driver for that summer wakeboarding weekend, or even a Bible teacher with a special area of interest or expertise who can teach for a week or two. I had the privilege of taking a group of students on a canoe trip with an expert outdoorsman who came with us for the five days we were on the river. He knew things about every bug, bird, and beast we encountered on that trip. Having him with us turned a routine paddle in the wilderness into a National Geographic documentary. He showed us things we couldn't possibly have seen on our own, and the kids who were on that trip will never forget him.

The one important thing to keep in mind when we work with these specialists is that we must position them for more than simply serving in their area of expertise. Their greatest contribution will be made relationally even as, in these other valued ways, they serve the students.

KEY PLAYERS

Now involvement begins to get more costly in terms of time and energy. As we move toward greater levels of commitment, we begin to think in terms of a weekly assignment that puts adults on a team and gives them a regular and intentional relationship with the students they serve. These are the people who are typically identified as being part of the visible, volunteer youth ministry staff. One of the most common ways to involve volunteers at this level is to invite them to consider becoming a small group leader or, if your ministry doesn't use small groups, to make them part of your weekly ministry team. These people are expected to be faithful in their attendance and participation and to intentionally develop ministry relationships with a group of students. If they're leading a small group, they'll be expected to be well prepared each week and to participate regularly in the training opportunities that are provided.

In most ministries this group of leaders represents the relational backbone of the team. They are strategically positioned in the lives of teens to walk with them over the course of time so they can make a significant investment in the individuals they connect with. Some leaders have found it's advantageous to assign these volunteers to a group of young teens—perhaps while still early in junior high—and then have them work with those students over the course of five or six years. Others change up the groups on an annual basis. Either way, these volunteers are challenged to build deep ministry friendships with students and to be available to them at a substantial level outside of the specific meeting times they're assigned to.

THE 110 PERCENTERS

Some ministries are fortunate enough to have a few core volunteers who are deeply involved in every aspect of ministry programming. They represent the deepest level of volunteer commitment. The blessing of having people who are willing to invest with this degree of dedication is immeasurable. They have a sense of the big picture and often function at all of the levels described above. They may be small group leaders who also serve as cooks and bus drivers when needed, willingly mentor a young person, and faithfully pray for the group. These are the people who can be counted on at the fund-raisers, service projects, and weekend retreats. They happily invite students to meet and offer to have them into their homes for dinner with their families or households; they offer availability to the kids who are hurting and need someone to listen to. Great care should be taken when working with these people to ensure that they are not taken advantage of or abused in their willingness to serve freely.

TRUTH FROM THE TRENCHES
Great care should be taken with those devoting themselves at the 110 percent level: ensure that they are not taken advantage of or abused in their willingness to serve freely.

APPRENTICES (INTERNS)

You may be fortunate enough to have the opportunity to invite team members into an even deeper level of ministry. You may be able to provide an extended supervised placement for men and women who want to seriously explore their call to youth ministry in an actual hands-on ministry environment. In most of these arrangements the expectation is that the work they do with students be viewed as their highest priority (as opposed to a job or full-time school responsibilities). At times a church or community will provide the individual with an opportunity for a part-time job to generate some income, but even when this is the case the work these people do with teens is their primary focus.

The term we've often used to describe these people is intern. I must admit that I've become somewhat uncomfortable with the connotations that this word often brings up. Too many churches and campus ministries have positioned these young leaders as a resource to be consumed rather than a kingdom investment to be poured into. For this reason, I think there is sense in looking at these folks as apprentices. Historically, the notion of an apprentice much more closely matches what is required to prepare someone for a vocation.

For an apprenticeship to be a useful experience there are several factors that must be present. The first, and by far the most important, is the quality of relationship between the mentor and the apprentice. In a very real sense the mentor is there to serve the apprentice as a model of excellence, a guide, an encourager, a corrector, and an advocate. When an apprenticeship involves learning with and from another person rather than simply being given a series of tasks to do, the experience is changed completely. Not only is a quality relationship with a supervisor important, the apprenticeship must take place over an extended period of time. To prepare well for all the relational challenges inherent in working with students and their families and to develop the basic competencies, an apprentice should experience at least a full year of a ministry's calendar. Those who can do two years describe it as even better.

Unfortunately, many small ministries don't believe they have what it takes to invest in an apprentice, or intern. Don't make that decision on the basis of size. If your people are committed to investing in the kingdom and you have a godly, experienced mentor available in your community, an apprentice (intern) might fit your situation perfectly. Check with colleges in your area to see if they have a young leader in mind whom you can invest in. Of course, the benefits will be mutual, but the deepest satisfaction will come from knowing that you've invested in a young leader who will make a significant difference with his or her life.

TRUTH FROM THE TRENCHES

To prepare well for all the relational challenges inherent in working with students and their families, an apprentice, or intern, should experience at least a full year of a ministry's calendar. Those who can do two years describe it as even better.

If we expect every volunteer to be at every event and involved in the lives of every student, we will quickly discover that recruitment is an impossible task. People will run when they see us coming. We've looked at six levels of involvement that provide opportunities for virtually everyone to have some role in caring for the students in your community. As you put your team together, it's important for everyone to know that these different opportunities exist. Each volunteer is expected to be fully dedicated and faithful in the various roles they've been willing to assume, even though that may represent widely differing time and energy commitments.

ACTION PLAN

★ How would you respond to a volunteer who gets upset because he or she is putting a much greater effort into their role than others who don't give as much time or aren't as freely available?

MAKING IT WORK: POPPING THE QUESTION

Once we've determined how many and what kind of people we're looking for, it's time to let people know that we need them. How do we communicate the opportunities that exist in our youth ministries in a way that will motivate people to join the team?

Obviously, there are several options available to us. They fall into two broad categories. The first method is what I call the broadcast approach. A general announcement is made letting people know that more youth ministry volunteers are needed and inviting others to consider joining the team. These announcements are often supplemented with posters, bulletin inserts, a recruitment table in the foyer after the Sunday service, an announcement on the home page of the Web site, and more efforts of the like. The idea is to get the word to as many people as quickly as possible and hope that by casting the net widely we'll snag a few good fish. Some people have called this the shotgun method to distinguish it from the "rifle" method that I'm about to describe—but somehow the idea of hunting these poor souls down still just doesn't work for me.

The second category of recruitment strategies is what I call the targeted approach. Specific individuals who have been recognized as having potential to be good youth ministry volunteers are approached one-on-one and invited to consider joining the team. These people are identified in a variety of ways. In some cases the youth ministry team leader does the work alone, constantly vigilant for new people who might work well with kids, or even old-timers around the church who might be ready for a change. Some leaders invite the students into the process, asking them who they think would make a good team member and then approaching people who are identified by the kids. Another strategy is to go to the volunteers who are already on the team and ask them if they know anyone who would do a good job on the team. Obviously, there are advantages and disadvantages with each of these strategies. Let's look at each and discover where their strengths and weaknesses lie.

THE BROADCAST METHOD
The up side

When an appeal for more youth workers is made to a congregation, it communicates that good things are happening in the youth department. The youth group is growing, or new programs that need new leaders are being added. It can generate some buzz and excitement in the congregation for members to realize that their youth ministry is on a roll. That is always a good thing! Furthermore, the broadcast method does cast a wide net and may identify some people that we would have never considered asking—either because we thought they were too busy, thought they had no interest in working with teens, or we simply didn't know them.

The down side

People who fish know that when they cast a wide net they often snag things they never intended to snag. This is the biggest problem with the broadcast method of recruitment. Inevitably, the first person who runs to the sign-up table with a big grin on their face is the last person you want working with the teenagers in your community. Of course, the problem is that once you've made an impassioned plea for more volunteers because of the great need that exists, it can become extremely awkward to say no to these eager but unsuitable candidates.

One way to minimize this problem is to announce that you're looking for applicants to be considered for a spot on the youth ministry team and that there is a considerable process that people will have to go through before being accepted into the role. But even with this caveat in place it can be difficult to say no to some people who believe they are God's gift to kids. A little later on we'll explore several specific causes for concern that we should be aware of as we determine people's suitability for working with kids.

One other caution that should be considered when using the broadcast method is that it can inadvertently communicate a desperate message that nearly anyone will work to fill the roles. This can devalue the work being done by people who are already on the team.

TRUTH FROM THE TRENCHES

The broadcast method can inadvertently communicate a desperate message that nearly anyone will work in filling the roles needing filled. This can devalue the work being done by people who are already on the team.

TARGETED RECRUITMENT—THE LEADER DECIDES

The up side

The leader of the team has a sense of the big picture: what sort of person is needed to balance the personality or gift mix and even which tasks represent the highest recruitment priorities. The leader has a vision for the future that involves adding new ministry initiatives and the people needed to make them work. Most of the people in the congregation simply don't see things from that perspective. Furthermore, the people who are being recruited to work on the team will ultimately report to the team leader. Compatibility and strong team chemistry are often much easier to achieve if the leader chooses who will be on his team. It avoids the awkwardness and misunderstanding that occurs when well-meaning people suggest names of potential volunteers who are unsuitable.

The down side

Even the best leaders can't possibly know everyone who might be a good fit for the team. Extra eyes are needed to identify potential team members. Not only that, but when a leader does all the recruiting alone without consulting anyone for their input, it can be construed as a power play. If the strongest links of loyalty are to the leader, this creates an unstable team dynamic. The goal is to create a web of loyal and loving relationships between team members so that the strength is broadly based and everyone is tied in together. This allows the team to model healthy community to the young people they serve.

TRUTH FROM THE TRENCHES

If the leader is the only one choosing team members, this creates strong links of loyalty to that leader, and thus an unstable team dynamic. The goal is to create a web of loyal and loving relationships on the entire leadership team.

TARGETED RECRUITMENT—THE STUDENTS DECIDE
The up side

Anyone who's ever tried to recruit a youth ministry volunteer will know that the biggest deterrent people have to saying yes is fear. Adults are afraid that kids won't like them, that they're not cool enough, that someone could do a better job, that they don't know enough about the Bible, that they don't like loud rock music, and a whole lot of other fears that makes them cautious to say yes. When a leader goes to a group of students to ask them who they think would make a great youth ministry volunteer and they identify the adults who will ultimately be invited to join the team, many of those fears are diminished. The students are now communicating that they like the person, that they are open to getting to know them better, and that a lot of those excuses often used to say no really don't matter. When the students themselves open the door, those awkward first few weeks or months are made far easier.

The other huge advantage, of course, is that students feel empowered when they're consulted on something as important as building the team. It acknowledges that they have a contribution to make and that they are worthy of being taken seriously.

The down side

Unfortunately, students are not always equipped with the best judgment when it comes to these sorts of matters. They may be attracted to an adult who is edgy and cool but has no spiritual substance to bring to the relationship. They are often attracted by external appearance and attitude rather than thinking about matters of the heart. (1 Samuel 16:7 is a classic verse to reference on this point.) In addition, the students will usually be unaware of the history or track record of an individual and simply not have the information necessary to make a wise decision on a matter of this importance.

Here's where it gets really tough for the leader who gives students a voice. When they identify someone who is clearly unsuitable for the job, it puts the leader in a very difficult spot. Often it would not be helpful or even appropriate to share with the students why that individual would be disqualified, and this whole process can raise more questions than it answers. Now students feel disenfranchised because they were invited into a conversation and, in their minds, not taken seriously. If someone else is added to the team, the students might make it difficult for that new leader to integrate simply because they want to show support for the leader they suggested, who ultimately was rejected.

TRUTH FROM THE TRENCHES

If students are invited into the recruitment process only to see their choices not honored—even for the best of reasons—it's easy for them to then feel disenfranchised. The feeling will be that they were asked to join a conversation and, in their minds, not taken seriously.

TARGETED RECRUITMENT—THE VOLUNTEERS DECIDE
The up side

In this strategy the volunteer team is invited to suggest additional members when expansion is needed. There are a number of advantages that are immediately apparent. Veteran volunteers are not intimidated or threatened by new team members because they have a voice in identifying who those new people will be. When current members participate in identifying new members, transitions tend to be smooth and new people are integrated without any major upheaval. Perhaps even more importantly, these experienced youth workers understand the agony and the ecstasy of working with kids. They know what kind of person will do well and they are able to promote the joys of youth ministry to potential recruits with a rich authenticity that comes from having done it themselves. They speak from personal experience when they tell their friends how much fun it is to be involved in the lives of teenagers. And of course, as was the case with students, volunteers feel empowered when they are invited into a conversation that involves changing the makeup of their team.

The down side

Remember how we talked two chapters ago about the danger of assembling a team of clones? One of the easiest ways of doing that is to let team members recruit their own friends. They'll very often surround themselves with people who have the same background, the same interests, and even the same temperaments. After a few rounds of expanding the team, everybody starts to look the same. Of course, we once again face the challenge of having to say no to someone who a team member thinks would do a great job and, once again, we may not be in a position of publicly declaring why that individual is unsuitable—particularly if the reasoning is at all subjective.

One further concern must be addressed here. When volunteers are involved in the recruitment process, there is potential for the team to become cliquish. While it's extremely important to have a team of adults who get along well and enjoy being with each other, it's easy to cross the line and find yourself in a place where the volunteers are giving more attention to their relationships with each other than to their relationships with the students. When this happens it can be very difficult for a leader to refocus the energy of the team on their primary agenda, which is to minister to kids.

ACTION PLAN

★ What is the most effective combination of recruitment strategies in your specific situation? Develop a workable recruitment plan for the next twelve months, including a timeline and names of responsible individuals.

HOW NOT TO MAKE IT WORK: RECIPES FOR DISASTER

We've made the point that not just anyone will make a good addition to your team. In the early stages of this book we talked at length about the kind of character qualities that are necessary to be effective in working well with teenagers. There is obviously a lot more to it than most people realize!

Before we move into some specifics on recruitment strategies and team-building methods, there's one more important conversation that needs to be had. We'll need to spend just a little time identifying some legitimate causes for concern that we might encounter as we talk with people about becoming involved on our team. Over the years I've discovered a few things about the kinds of people who often don't work out well. If you can be aware of some of these tendencies before you get too far down the road with people, you may be able to save yourself a lot of headaches.

QUITTERS

These are people who have repeatedly demonstrated an inability to finish well. They have a long history of short-term commitments, most of which have not ended happily. Too often it seems that the end of their ministries is marked by unresolved conflict and misunderstandings—and they'll explain to you how, in each case, they were the victim. For others, their commitment just fizzles over time. They got bored, distracted, or too busy, and the motivation to remain faithful is lost. The interesting thing about these folks is that they often appear extremely eager at the beginning, but it's not long before that enthusiasm starts to wane, their attendance and participation become sporadic and unpredictable, and eventually they just disappear. It's obvious how destructive this can be to a group of teenagers looking for trustworthy nonparental adults in their lives.

By the way, it's a good idea to be just a little cautious when recruiting people who have recently begun attending your church. They may have a pattern of bouncing from one faith community to another, and until you understand the circumstances that caused them to leave, it's best not to put them into significant roles of leadership, especially with vulnerable young people. Give them an opportunity to put down some roots and demonstrate their commitment to your congregation and *then* think about involving them on your team.

NEW BELIEVERS

Of course, we want to do everything we can to get a new believer off to a good start in their walk of faith, but we should be cautious about pushing them too quickly into positions of leadership, particularly if those roles involve teaching or discipleship. The highest priority when dealing with baby Christians is to help them become deeply rooted and well established in their own personal journey before they're given a platform of ministry. What often happens is that because their focus is on the spiritual lives of others—in this case the group of teenagers they are leading—they don't have the time (or perhaps even the interest) to invest in their own walk with God.

A specific danger related to this issue of integrating new believers has to do with giving them rock star status because of the dramatic nature of their conversion story. It's often a temptation to put these new Christians in the spotlight, allowing them to tell their tale as something akin to celebrities, often with an inappropriate emphasis on the past. This reinforces all the wrong values for both the new believer and the young people in the audience. This is not to say that we shouldn't appropriately celebrate the spiritual transformations that God works in the lives of people (and the angels are dancing!, as Luke 15 tells us), but let's make sure that when the story is told, it is unapologetically God's story—not theirs.

TRUTH FROM THE TRENCHES

It's often a temptation to put new Christians who are doing well in the spotlight of ministry leadership. This can allow them to tell their tale as something akin to celebrities, often with an inappropriate emphasis on the past. This reinforces all the wrong values for both the new believer and the young people in the audience.

LIFE IN UPHEAVAL

Each of us can look back to key transitional times in our lives when things were in chaos: perhaps our college graduation year with its final exams, job searches, and a move across the country; the year we got married, with all of the adjustments that had to be made; bringing home a new baby and completely rethinking the schedule of each day. On a more somber note, some of us have experienced having someone near us die, going through a divorce or separation, losing our job, or other things of this nature. When people are going through traumatic, life-changing circumstances, it's often not wise to thrust them into a significant ministry role.

Of course, if people are already on the team and they encounter the sort of circumstances listed above, we embrace and support them through the upheaval and care for them as intentionally as we can. But to put someone in an important relational ministry role when everything around them is unpredictable and in turmoil simply adds one more layer of stress. My strong suggestion is that we give things an appropriate length of time to settle—at least a year in most cases—and then reopen the conversation to discover if there is a new level of readiness.

TRUTH FROM THE TRENCHES

To put someone into an important relational ministry role when everything around them is unpredictable and in turmoil will simply add one more layer of stress to their lives, and likely not serve your ministry well.

SOCIAL MISFITS

If you've built your team well, it will be obvious to everyone that your people love each other, enjoy what they do, and have a lot of fun together. The creativity, laughter, and camaraderie are attractive, especially to people who struggle socially. They may look at your group and long for what they see there. But of course, as all of us know, social interaction and adult friendships are not the reasons we get involved in youth ministry. It's for, and all about, the students—and what creates the wonderfully collaborative atmosphere is the fact that each team member is equally committed to that youth ministry purpose.

If you get the sense that there is any self-serving motivation for anyone who shows an interest in getting involved in youth ministry, red flags should be waving everywhere. I'm not saying that people shouldn't be attracted to the community aspect of working with people, but when you get the sense that this is the primary purpose for involvement, it's best to say no.

There may be an even greater concern when it comes to dealing with socially awkward individuals. Some of these people feel highly threatened in relationships with same-age peers and often pursue relationships with younger people because they feel relationally safer with them than with adults. Again, this represents a significant cause for concern. You want people on your team who are entirely comfortable in mature relationships. In fact, one of the things you need to monitor is that your most highly motivated volunteers are spending time socially with same-age peers who have nothing to do with youth ministry.

POLITICIANS AND PLATFORM SEEKERS

May God give you wisdom and discernment! Sometimes it's very difficult to identify people with a political purpose or the need for a platform before it's too late. Hidden agendas for power, control, or even political gain often drive people in churches to seek leadership positions. They may appear to be benign and cooperative when they volunteer to help, but it doesn't take long to realize that there was something else driving their benevolence.

I'll never forget how hard it was to get rid of an ultraconservative woman who felt that it was her job to rescue a generation of young people from what she considered to be the inappropriate theology being taught from the pulpit. She volunteered to take on a small group, but instead of leading them to an understanding of truth in the Scripture, she spent all her time critiquing and undermining the rest of the ministry of the church. It was divisive and inappropriate and, of course, when she was challenged, it made her a martyr.

I've seen people volunteer for youth ministry so that they can find firsthand evidence for getting a youth pastor fired. I've seen them join the team because they disagree with the youth ministry philosophy and believe they can change it from the inside out. The list could go on and on, but I think the point is clear. It's about loving students in Jesus' name and pointing them to the truth. Selfish motives destroy teams.

TRUTH FROM THE TRENCHES

The bottom line with youth ministry and those who want to be on your teams: The ministry is about loving students in Jesus' name and pointing them to the truth. Selfish motives destroy teams.

GRAY ZONE DWELLERS

Youth workers are role models whether they like it or not. We serve a generation that listens with its eyes. Your most significant instrument of ministry is your life, lived visibly so that a young generation can see the difference that the gospel makes in you. This means that youth ministry team members may be legitimately called to a higher standard in areas of lifestyle, behavior, habits, relationships, and choices. I'm not talking about living hypocritically or maintaining a double standard. I'm talking about consciously recognizing that teens are watching, and making choices to live above reproach in every area of life.

Beware of recruiting adults who are not consciously pursuing a life of holiness. Our young people need to see models of spiritual discipline and chosen obedience. Galatians 5 addresses this issue when it lists evidences of living by our sinful nature. It talks about things like sexual immorality, impurity, idolatry, and witchcraft; hatred, discord, jealousy, fits of rage, selfish ambition, dissensions, factions, envy, drunkenness, orgies, and more (Galatians 5:19-21). In contrast, we're looking for people whose lives consistently reflect the fruit of the Spirit—manifestations like love, joy, peace, patience, and kindness (Galatians 5:22, 23). It's your responsibility as a leader to remind your team that they are living their lives before young people who are often looking for ways to justify their own gray area of choices. It's a fine line, but one certainly worth discussing and defining. Individuals whose lifestyle choices will give students an excuse to live carelessly don't make good youth workers.

But the fruit of the Spirit is love, joy, peace, patience, kindness, goodness, faithfulness, gentleness and self-control. Against such things there is no law.

GALATIANS 5:22, 23

LACKING SUPPORT FROM THE FAMILY

Because of the intensely relational nature of youth ministry, it's pretty important to have the full support of the people who are closest to your team members. If they're married they need to have the support of their spouse. This doesn't mean that both husband and wife must be formally involved in youth ministry (although there are some wonderful advantages to having husband-wife teams involved). But an unsupportive spouse can create major problems for someone who is committed to youth ministry and for the team as a whole. It's important for you as a leader to take the time to discover what the concern of the spouse might be and then to determine how that concern could be addressed. In most cases it will revolve around issues of over-commitment, rearranged priorities, and fear. In most cases, if these factors cannot be appropriately addressed, it is better to rethink the role the individual might play.

One solution might be to drop their level of involvement to something that requires less time and energy and still allows them to have a role in the life of a student. For example, a spouse may be reluctant about hosting a weekly small group meeting in their house, but would be entirely comfortable with their partner as a mentor. The one place where this becomes a particularly thorny issue is when we're dealing with an individual who is married to someone who is not a believer and is uncooperative about every aspect of their partner's spiritual life. Each of these cases needs to be addressed individually, but as a general rule, if involvement on the team will be destructive to a home or a marriage, it's better to say no to that person being on your team.

THE PROS AND CONS OF PARENTS AS YOUTH MINISTRY VOLUNTEERS

I've had some of my best and some of my worst experiences in ministry when I've recruited parents of teenagers to be volunteers. When the experience was positive, it was because I was dealing with people who had a legitimately vested interest in providing a strong youth ministry program for their own sons and daughters. They understood teenagers because they lived with them. The loud music, late nights, bottomless appetites, peculiar smells, emotional roller coasters, and constantly changing friendship clusters were not strange or intimidating. They had a great relationship with their own teens, so no one felt threatened by their presence on the team. They were committed to the overall spiritual growth of all the members in the group and their contribution was positive in every way. In short, it can work, and it can work well.

But it's also instructive to contrast those pictures with a few disastrous parents-as-volunteers experiences. They either over-parented or under-parented their own kids to the point where it became awkward for everyone. They were not there for the good of the whole group and were often far more critical than supporting. It was almost impossible for them to be objective about even the simplest decisions that the team had to make because everything was determined by how it would impact their child. They dealt condescendingly with younger youth workers, declaring them to be naive and lacking experience: "Just wait till you have kids of your own—then you'll understand what the rest of us are going through."

So how do we use parents in youth ministry well? Entire books have been written on this subject, and a great one is a companion book in this series, *Engaging Parents as Allies,* by Wayne Rice. (I wrote another; if you want more of my thoughts on this topic, have a look at *Youth Worker's Guide to Parent Ministry,* published by Zondervan in 2003.) The secret, essentially, is to make sure that everybody is on the same page. Parents need to understand that if they join the team they do so with the same expectations as anyone else who's there. Teenagers need to be comfortable with their parents at youth group; I always give the teens the first right of refusal. If they don't want their mom and dad there, mom and dad aren't on the team. Again, the principle of ensuring that no volunteer is driven by a self-serving motivation is at the heart of this decision.

One of the ways parents who are genuinely interested in doing youth ministry (but who don't want to be involved in the same group as their teenage sons and daughters) can serve is to simply put them in the opposite age group from where their children are. For example, parents of junior high or middle school students can serve on the senior high team, or vice versa. Just make sure you've carefully thought through the full implications of involving parents in leadership roles before you appoint them to important team ministry positions.

ACTION PLAN

★ This chapter raises eight areas of concern that should be carefully considered in the recruiting process. Which of these are absolute deal breakers? For each of the others, think about how you would respond if an individual with this characteristic volunteers to join the team. What changes would need to be in place before they would be considered?

MAKING IT WORK: TEAM BUILDING 101—STEPS TO SUCCESS

I t has probably occurred to you by this time that a good recruitment plan will use a combination of methods and target a wide range of potential leaders. Because we're inviting people to be involved at a number of different levels, it will be important to utilize the most appropriate strategy in each case. For example, it would be perfectly OK to recruit people for the prayer team using the broadcast method, but mentors would likely require a much more targeted approach. Regardless of which level of involvement you're recruiting people for, it must be done with excellence, intentionality, and care. If your approach is slipshod and haphazard, people will not take you or the ministry they are being invited to consider seriously.

There is one more important reminder that must be reemphasized. You are not asking these individuals to fill a slot that you need filled. This isn't about propping up a program that is short-staffed and failing as a result. The intention is not to create a platform for guilt, coercion, or manipulation. The purpose is to assist each individual in your faith community in finding a satisfying place to serve. It's about helping people discern their passions, spiritual gifts, and ministry desires and then matching those with the opportunities—you'll notice I didn't use the word *needs*—that are available within the youth ministry program. It's helping people find an excellent fit.

Before we go any further, let me concede that you should be suspicious any time you see a list of steps in a book on ministry, especially when they are identified as "Steps to Success." We all know that life is messier than that. I'm not suggesting in what follows that a rigid, structured approach is the only way to build your team. In fact, everything you read in this book needs to be adapted and applied with flexibility and sensitivity to your unique situation. What I *am* suggesting is that you need a plan.

What follows is a general overview of the recruitment process that has evolved in my own ministry experience over the course of time. I should say that I don't follow these rules without exception in every instance. However, I have learned that the closer I stick to my plan the more likely I am to have successful outcomes. Consider these steps to be a suggested process to model what a successful plan might look like. If you feel like these steps have the potential to guide you in your team building, please feel free to use them as is. If you need to adapt them and make them your own, I'm happy to have jump-started your thinking about how you can be more effective in putting together a team.

TRUTH FROM THE TRENCHES

The closer you stick to your recruitment plan the more likely you are to have successful outcomes.

STEP ONE: DEVELOP A STRONG ROLE DESCRIPTION FOR EACH MINISTRY POSITION

Every youth ministry is unique in its philosophy, leadership structure, and program particulars. That means that each ministry will have its own list of positions and staffing needs. In addition to small group leaders and Sunday school teachers, I've seen youth groups with prayer coordinators, worship leaders, media and tech staff, advertising and promotion coordinators, treasurers, snack captains, Web designers, recreation directors, PowerPoint operators, mission trip chaperones, and lots of other program-specific designations.

Imagine the benefit it would be to each of these individuals if they had a clearly stated role description that communicated the details of their assigned function on the team. They would know to whom they reported, where to get the resources necessary to complete their task, how their involvement contributed to the overall mission of the youth department, the expected schedule, and even the basis upon which their role would be evaluated. (Find a sample role description in Appendix 1 to this book.) After talking to hundreds of volunteers over the years, my sense is that their greatest frustration is in not knowing what is expected of them and thus having no basis upon which to evaluate their own effectiveness. A role description gives credence and significance to both the individual who takes a task on and to the task itself.

STEP TWO: IDENTIFY SUITABLE INDIVIDUALS TO BE CONSIDERED FOR EACH ROLE

We talked in chapter 8 about the various ways individuals can be identified for youth ministry roles. As you begin to think about who might be a good fit, it's important to look at the full range of commitment levels that are available as well as the various methods for recruiting individuals. If you use the broadcast method to communicate your need for additional volunteer staff, be extremely careful not to communicate that availability automatically guarantees a role. Instead, always speak in terms of inviting people to apply for a position, then reminding them that there are a number of steps that must be undertaken before an appointment is made. If you're consulting youth group students or current volunteers for their suggestions as to who might be suitable, be sure you communicate the same thing to them. Their suggestions do not automatically guarantee their friend an invitation to serve. The important thing is that in most circumstances students and current volunteers should not be the ones who do the inviting. That responsibility should be left to the youth ministry point person—the ministry leader, whether that person is paid or volunteer.

TRUTH FROM THE TRENCHES

In most circumstances, neither ministry leadership volunteers nor students should do the job of inviting new people onto the team. The ministry leader should take that responsibility.

STEP THREE: MAKE AN APPOINTMENT TO PRESENT THE MINISTRY OPPORTUNITY

Once an individual has been identified as suitable, it's important to arrange to have a purposeful conversation with that person. The key word here is *purposeful*. Setting up an actual appointment helps the person realize that this is a serious request being made and that you respect their time and their need to process the opportunity carefully. Far too much youth ministry recruitment is done in church parking lots without much thought or preparation given. When someone is invited to consider a serious ministry commitment during a spontaneous conversation in the church foyer, it's far too easy for them to thoughtlessly say either yes or no. We're not talking about a scavenger hunt with a time limit here.

When an individual is approached, the agenda should be clear and the purpose of the conversation should be stated upfront. Beware of the bait and switch. I'd suggest you simply say something like: "We're inviting some new people to consider the possibility of joining our youth ministry volunteer team. As we've been talking with the students your name has come up as someone that they see being well suited for the team. They've asked me if I would talk to you and invite you to consider hearing more about the opportunity. When can I buy you a coffee so I can tell you more about what would be involved in this position?" An introduction like this will open the door to an honest discussion. The intention is clear and there are no surprises. It models the kind of integrity that should mark your entire approach to ministry.

STEP FOUR: MEET ONE-ON-ONE TO INVITE INVOLVEMENT AND EXPLAIN THE VETTING PROCESS

Prepare for your meeting by praying that God will give you discernment and wisdom as you talk about how this individual might fit into the ministry team. Make sure you are fully conversant in the details of the role you're inviting them to consider. This includes all the details that should be found on the printed role description that you bring with you: role title, role overview, qualifications, reporting lines, anticipated time commitment, schedules and dates, available resources and training, and details of the application process. It's important for the person you're talking with to realize that there will be a few steps involved here, including an application form, an interview of some type, and a mandatory background check for any youth workers who have direct contact with students.

Begin your conversation by indicating that your desire is to help this person find a satisfying and joy-filled place to serve in the community. Affirm what you believe makes them suitable for the role. Help them understand the larger vision for youth ministry and how their proposed role contributes to that overall vision. Give them opportunity to ask any questions they might have. Do not ask for an immediate response to your invitation. It's important to give them time to think and pray about what they're considering committing to, to discuss it with their spouse or their own children (if they have them), and to learn a bit more about what their role will involve.

I recognize that this process sounds serious and formal—especially if you've been trying to recruit people as they're walking out the door of the church on Sunday morning. But the intentional nature of this process provides a much more solid start—even if you could have gotten the person you have in mind to say yes without going through the steps.

TRUTH FROM THE TRENCHES

It's important to give the person you're inviting onto the team time to think and pray about what they're considering committing to, to discuss it with their spouse or their own children (if they have them), and to learn a bit more about what their role will involve.

STEP FIVE: INVITE THEM TO PARTICIPATE IN A SAMPLE EVENT

Whether people are enthusiastic or reluctant regarding getting involved, it's always a good idea to give them a taste of what youth ministry is like before they commit to applying formally (or flatly turn you down). Invite them to come along as an observer to an upcoming event. This will give them an opportunity to see the existing team in action, to get a sense of who the teens are, and to get a feel for the overall ethos of the youth group. Most of us know that once people have spent a little time in the same room with teens, heard their laughter, seen them interacting with one another, and sensed the need for adults to be involved in their lives, they'll know if they are called to this ministry or not. If individuals are being asked to consider a specific role such as that of a Sunday school teacher or small group leader, it's entirely appropriate for them to be invited to observe that specific ministry in action. Debrief their experience by asking for their feedback and seeing if they have any questions.

STEP SIX: GIVE THEM TIME TO CONSIDER, DISCUSS, AND PRAY ABOUT YOUR INVITATION

This step is not just the clichéd and predictable "right thing to do." When we invite people to carefully consider and pray about their involvement, we're acknowledging the significance of the role we're inviting them to. This is spiritual work, and for people to succeed long-term there must be a sense of being called to the position. Establish a time frame for this process. Let the person know when you'll get back to them looking for a response, and then assure them that you'll be praying with them that they will clearly sense God's direction regarding this invitation.

STEP SEVEN: DO THE PAPERWORK

Once someone has indicated a willingness to move forward, the formal application process can begin. Have them start by filling out the application form you have prepared. (A sample form is in Appendix 2.) In addition to the contact information you will gather there, it gives the person an opportunity to articulate some things about their own faith journey and to affirm their sense of call to this ministry. As you go through their form, you'll discover some things about these people that you might not have discovered any other way: unique skills, hobbies, areas of interest, education and training, and other details that will help you position them for ministry success. At this point, an interview may seem like overkill with people you already know well, but the purpose is not only to screen them but also to hear their hearts, to answer any final questions they might have, to pray with them, and to talk about how they would be oriented and integrated into the ministry.

The final step is to have them participate in a background check that legally clears them to be involved with children and young people. Even if you're doing your recruiting in a community where background checks are not yet mandatory, I would strongly suggest that you do them—and not only on new volunteers but on your existing team as well. It's not to be paranoid or untrusting. Instead, the purpose is to set a precedent in which everyone is subject to the same process. If this policy is not in place and you find yourself dealing with an applicant who does create suspicion, it becomes extremely awkward to impose the background check on one person. On the other hand, if everyone goes through this process there is no misunderstanding. Not only that, but should you find yourself in a position where the safety of your young people has been compromised and you need to prove your diligence, you'll be much further ahead legally if this policy has been in place. In most communities the background check is conducted through the police department and involves a small fee for its administration. It often takes several weeks for the paperwork to be completed, so be prepared for some administrative stuff to be involved in this process. If one of your existing volunteers or a new recruit balks at the notion of a background check, it may be an indication that they won't do well in youth ministry. The safety of our teens has to be everyone's highest priority.

TRUTH FROM THE TRENCHES

You should consider background checks all but mandatory for your ministry. The purpose is to set a precedent in which everyone is subject to the same process. The safety of our teens has to be everyone's highest priority.

STEP EIGHT: INVOLVE THE NEW VOLUNTEER IN A TRAINING OR PLANNING MEETING AT THE FIRST CHANCE

It's important to integrate your new recruits as soon as possible. A great way to show them that you're committed to walking with them in their ministry is to invite them to a training event as soon as possible. We'll talk more specifically about training volunteers in chapter 12, but at this point let me say that you should be offering regular training sessions for all your volunteers, so scheduling, and their attendance at one, shouldn't be too difficult. This is also a great way for your new team members to integrate with the existing team without students being present. As we've already discussed, building strong relationships on the team is a high priority.

ACTION PLAN

★ How can you adapt this eight-step process to your ministry? Do you do a number of these steps already? How might implementing the steps not being used in your ministry be helpful?

uilding a team is as much art as science. Following the steps that were outlined in chapter 10 will get you off to a pretty good start and eliminate a lot of the problems we often face as team builders. Doing it right has some huge benefits. When the process is carefully undertaken, surprises are reduced, expectations are realistic, important questions are answered, and the potential for a long-term ministry is substantially strengthened.

But there are some other lessons I've learned about recruiting that just don't fit neatly into a series of steps. Most of these have been learned by mistake, and my hope is that by sharing some of these principles you can avoid some of the blunders I've made along the way.

START EARLY

Twisting someone's arm for "this weekend" or "next Wednesday" communicates all the wrong things about the youth ministry and the value we place on people. Sadly, much of the recruitment that takes place in churches falls into this frantic, urgent category and reinforces the notion that leaders are simply desperate to fill slots. The stress this approach puts on the leader is only matched by the guilt it puts on the person who has to say no. It's simply not the way the kingdom of God was meant to be built.

A six-to-nine-month window from the time of the initial conversation to the time when someone is actually fully trained for ministry is not at all unreasonable. It allows the conversations to be leisurely rather than rushed. The application and background check process can run its course without being hurried or short-circuited. People are given time to make adjustments to their own schedules and other ministry obligations so that they can give their full attention to the new responsibilities they are committing to. It also provides time for orientation and training for the new volunteer. If you hope to see an individual ready to serve in the fall, the time to begin the conversation is early in the new year.

CHALLENGE PEOPLE TO CHOOSE

Most of us who've been around the church are aware of the 80/20 rule. It cynically quantifies a trend that often marks the way ministry responsibilities are divided up in too many congregations by suggesting that 80 percent of the work is done by 20 percent of the people. Of course, this means that the willing are often wearing multiple ministry hats. One person might head up the Sunday school, sing in a worship team, serve on a search committee, lead a Bible study in her home, and direct the Christmas pageant. And now she feels called to youth ministry!

Beware of eager servants who have overcommitted to the point of jeopardizing their own spiritual health and the well-being of their families "for the sake of the kingdom." Not only do they eventually find themselves unable to juggle all their responsibilities, they also model all the wrong things to the young people to whom they'll be teaching lessons about healthy living. Because youth ministry is relational rather than programmatic, it simply does not lend itself well to people dropping in at the last minute, doing their job, and then running off to their next responsibility. This is where the issue of true availability—discussed in the early pages of this book—becomes such an important concept.

Many churches have found that reducing the number of major responsibilities given to each person makes life a little easier for everyone. It would not be unreasonable for you to ask potential volunteers to restrict their ministry involvement to youth ministry as their major investment and then to allow a minor role or two in other areas as a way of expressing some of their other gifts. We're talking about leadership in your ministry, not just participation. We're not restricting people's involvement in a Bible study or forbidding them from taking a role in the pageant, but simply asking them to be cautious about how many major responsibilities they take on.

ASK FOR A ONE-YEAR COMMITMENT AT A TIME

The biggest fear most people have when they commit themselves to a leadership role in the church is that they've just voluntarily given themselves a life sentence. In a ministry environment where filling job slots is the priority, it's almost impossible to get out of a responsibility once you have it. Of course, we all know that there is great value in people being involved long-term in most volunteer positions. This is especially true in the relational world of working with students. A revolving door of volunteers coming and going erodes trust and undermines the stability of the team.

Having said those things, my experience has been that the best way to keep people for the long haul is to assure them that they are not trapped. Asking people to commit for one year at a time and then giving them the opportunity to reevaluate annually keeps their commitment fresh and focused. There is nothing that will kill the spirit of a team more quickly than a group of people who are serving purely out of obligation and guilt, believing that they have no option but to keep on keeping on. On a practical note, the conversation about a new annual commitment should typically happen three or four months before the new term of service is meant to begin. That gives you time to replace people who may feel it's time to move on.

TRUTH FROM THE TRENCHES

The best way to keep people for the long haul is to assure them that they are not trapped. Ask people to commit for one year at a time and then give them the opportunity to reevaluate annually; this keeps their commitment fresh and focused.

RECRUIT ALL YEAR LONG

Most church programs kick off in the fall. That means the summer often becomes a peak recruiting season. But truthfully, I can't think of a worse time to contact people and secure a commitment. Families are on vacation, attendance may be sporadic, and people are trying to put off thinking about the fall. We've already talked about the importance of starting early. Because our groups grow all year long, it's not a bad idea to look for potential youth workers all year long as well. The biggest advantage is that you're not trying to integrate a lot of new leaders all at once. It's so much easier to bring them on one at a time, help them find their place in the ministry, and let the students get used to one or two new people at a time. The truth of the matter is that a good youth ministry leader should be constantly thinking about how to build and strengthen the team. It's not just seasonal work.

TRUTH FROM THE TRENCHES

A good youth ministry leader should be constantly thinking about how to build and strengthen the team. It's not just seasonal work.

BUILD IN A PROBATION PERIOD

Even the most careful application and vetting process doesn't eliminate all the uncertainties and surprises that might arise. I've been astounded on too many occasions at how badly mistaken I was about someone's suitability for youth ministry. Usually it quickly became clear to me that this wasn't going to work and that I would have to find a gracious way to ask someone to step aside. In most of those cases the individual was blissfully unaware of how poorly things were working out. By contrast, in some other situations, I was the one who was oblivious to how little joy the person was finding in their new responsibilities. Either way, an awkward conversation had to happen.

A well-defined probationary period, or trial run, opens the door for a frank conversation early on in a volunteer's ministry journey and can provide a less painful escape for both parties if it becomes necessary. My suggestion would be to schedule a first evaluation meeting at about the three-month point. By that time both of you should have a pretty good sense of how things are going. If some adjustments or corrections are necessary, this is a good time to intro-duce them. If all the volunteer needs at this stage is encouragement, it's a great time to provide them with that. And of course, if it's become evident that it's not working at all, the earlier we can take steps to change things the less damage that will occur.

At a minimum, a second meeting should be scheduled at about the nine-month point to discuss plans for the following year. Assuming things are going well, this will give you an opportunity to invite the team member into another year of ministry. If things are not going well, the end of a year is a great time to part ways without all sorts of explanations being necessary. The issue of firing (or *releasing*, if we need a euphemism) volunteers will be discussed in more detail in our final chapter, but that's a slightly different topic than processing a volunteer's probation.

TRUTH FROM THE TRENCHES

A well-defined probationary period opens the door for a frank conversation early on in a volunteer's ministry journey and can provide a less painful escape for both parties if it becomes necessary.

MAKE THEM MORE THAN CHAUFFEURS, CHEFS, AND CHAPERONES

In spite of the fact that each team member will have an assigned task—leading a group, serving snacks, heading up the welcoming team, driving the bus, etc.—they must understand that their primary function is relational. The roles we give them are crucial ones in and of themselves, but on the more important level, they are really nothing more than excuses to hang around the students so they can develop life-on-life ministries. Help your volunteers understand this principle by consistently evaluating their effectiveness in relational terms:

- ★ Affirm the camp cook for the great rapport she has with the kids who are in the kitchen helping her with the dishes.
- ★ Applaud the bus driver for getting to know the names of each of the students on the retreat.
- ★ Challenge the small group leader to make at least one informal contact with each of the teens in his group each week.
- ★ If there's a large group event happening, encourage your adult volunteers to mingle with the group rather than forming a wall of humanity around the outside.

Be sure to model the primary importance of relationship in the way you interact with students as the leader of the youth ministry. If we believe it's all about relationship, that conviction must be evident in every aspect of a volunteer's experience.

DELEGATE AUTHORITY WHEN YOU DELEGATE RESPONSIBILITY

There's nothing more frustrating for a volunteer than to be given responsibility for an aspect of ministry without being given the authority to make the necessary decisions to accomplish the task. This is one of the biggest mistakes that young, inexperienced, or power-hungry leaders make. Sadly, in many cases, it's the latter of the three. The leader off-loads the task on one of the team members and assumes a level of performance and excellence but then insists that any decisions relating to the accomplishment of that task must come back for approval. Whether we're talking about the power-hungry or the inexperienced leader, what drives this pattern is almost always a need for control, a lack of trust, and the fear of failure.

When volunteers or other team members are given responsibility for a task, they need two things to be successful. The first is a clear understanding of where the necessary resources are to be found, and the second is the authority to make decisions, especially when things don't go exactly as planned. A team that is empowered to carry out its assignments without constantly having to check back with the leader is a team that is energetic and highly motivated. A leader who is not constantly checking up on his people because he doesn't trust them is a leader who can invest energy in encouraging, resourcing, and caring for his team. Leaders must constantly ask themselves if this team could function without them.

TRUTH FROM THE TRENCHES

A leader who is not constantly checking up on his people because he doesn't trust them is a leader who can invest energy in encouraging, resourcing, and caring for his team.

ACTION PLAN

★ Most of us have been both recruits and recruiters at various times. As you look back on the teams you've been a part of, what are some of the mistakes you've made or been subjected to? What are some of the things you've done right?

MAKING IT WORK: A HAPPY TEAM FOR THE LONG HAUL

The principles and practices we've discussed to this point in this book will help you assemble a team of people you should be able to count on. You've been clear on what is expected of them in the invitation process, you've taken the time to determine that their hearts for ministry are prepared to serve, and you've established a team atmosphere that makes people want to be there. But none of that matters if you're not giving careful attention to the week-by-week leadership of that team by consistently providing for them what they need to be successful.

LEARN TO DELEGATE WELL

Sprinters on a relay team know that next to running really fast, the most important skill they need to work on is handing off the baton well. In fact, it really doesn't matter how fast they can run if the little stick is dropped in that crucial moment. Football quarterbacks live with the same reality. How many long marches down the field have ended with a fumbled handoff? And for a youth ministry team leader, how many amazing program ideas and ministry opportunities have tanked simply because they weren't delegated well?

The great value in building a solid team is that the responsibilities of ministry can be spread broadly over the shoulders of many people. This means that tasks need to be doled out according to the level of commitment, passions, and gifts of individual team members. But giving someone a task that matches in those three areas doesn't necessarily guarantee success. The delegation process must be done intentionally and carefully or it will be doomed to failure. How do we hand over responsibility well?

A classic delegation model has been floating around for as long as I've been in youth ministry and probably most readers are familiar with it. It's a simple four-step plan and my experience has been that when I follow it, the delegation process is pleasant and free of anxiety. On the other hand, when I fail to do it this way, I often end up frustrated and disappointed.

Step one: I do it and you watch

In this preliminary stage the leader models the task or skill that will be delegated. The purpose is to show how it is meant to be done and to set the expected standard. The key is to make the potential new leader aware of the fact that the skill is being demonstrated with delegation in mind.

Step two: I do it and you help

Now the leader is invited into the process and given the opportunity to become much more than a mere observer. Gradually, she is invited in to the task itself, assisting the leader while the new skills are being learned. Depending on how complex the task being delegated is, this step could take a considerable amount of time. The important thing at this stage is that the burden of responsibility remains with the teacher rather than the learner.

Step three: You do it and I help

It's now time for the responsibility to be shifted to the new leader. The apprentice has by this time experienced every aspect of the new responsibility under the guidance of the teacher. There have been opportunities to have questions answered and skills refined. As the new leader takes on more and more responsibility, the teacher steps back, allowing the rookie to gain confidence, while the teacher encourages and gently corrects each step of the way.

Step four: You do it and I do something else

When both the teacher and the apprentice are confident that the task can be performed at the expected level of quality, the goal of delegation has been achieved. The rookie is experiencing the joy of accomplishing something significant in ministry, and the teacher is able to move on and give attention to some other area of responsibility.

As you read these simple steps, I know that some of you are looking for your "D" file so you can put this under DUH! But before you rush ahead assuming you've heard all this before, let me ask you: When was the last time you actually followed this plan? It's one of those things that we all know about but rarely have the time or energy to do right. Fortunately, for many leaders, this process is almost instinctive and their confident and well-equipped volunteers are visible evidence that it really does work.

GENEROUSLY PROVIDE TOOLS AND RESOURCES

The past decade has been marked by a proliferation of outstanding youth ministry tools and resources. Practical books have been written by youth ministry veterans. Well-developed curriculum is available for every age group on virtually every biblical topic one can think of. Electronic resources, video clips, online libraries, DVDs and CD-ROMs, and more are available to make the work of a volunteer youth worker manageable.

It's the responsibility of the team leader to make these many resources available to the volunteer team so that their hands will be strengthened, and that any extra energy they may have can be funneled into relationships rather than building programs from scratch. The good news is that these resources are relatively easy to find and make available to your team. A quick online search of key words like "youth ministry curriculum," "youth ministry ideas," "youth group games," "help hurting kids," and dozens of others will make a world of excellent tools quickly available. In addition to all the resources available for purchase, or simply available on the Web, it's a good idea to be intentional about developing a solid hands-on library of youth ministry books and curriculum.

We place a great deal of responsibility on our volunteer team and expect that they do their ministry with excellence and creativity. One of the best ways we can ensure high standards is to make the necessary tools available to them.

TRUTH FROM THE TRENCHES

To help our volunteer leaders do their ministry with excellence and creativity, we need to ensure high standards and make the necessary tools available to them.

KEEP IT AFFORDABLE

Youth ministry volunteers serve at considerable cost. They give up family time, social interaction with their peers, personal free time, and often their own comfort and privacy for the sake of being available to the teenagers of their community. If there is any way that you can reduce the financial costs involved, it will go a long way toward keeping them on your team for the long haul. For those who have young children, this could involve something as simple as providing free babysitting or child care during the times they're involved in youth activities. It might also include structuring your budget so that volunteers don't have to pay their own way when there is a weekend retreat, or concert, or even a bowling night for that matter. Some ministry budgets are even designed to subsidize the food costs and Coke date expenses that volunteers may incur in their ministry relationships with teens. The point is that we want to make volunteering as stress-free as possible, and for some people the financial component of it can be enough to push them away.

OFFER REGULAR TRAINING OPPORTUNITIES

Another key factor in keeping your volunteers motivated and effective over the long haul is to ensure that they're given regular opportunities to sharpen their skills through a comprehensive training program. We've already discussed the importance of orienting and training people at the beginning, just after they've been recruited, but now we're talking about an ongoing training program for the whole team. When we invest in our people this way, it communicates to them the value we place on the work they do, bonds them as a team, and builds their confidence as they implement the information they receive.

The most common approach to team building and training is to invite the whole team to gather on some sort of a regular basis—monthly or quarterly— to deal with any topics pertinent to all of them. In most cases, the leader prepares material based on perceived areas of weakness, a specific issue that has come up, or a comprehensive training plan that has been prepared ahead of time. I strongly suggest the implementation of this sort of regular ministry development, but there are other ways that training can happen as well.

TRUTH FROM THE TRENCHES

When we invest in our people with intentional, long-term training, it communicates to them the value we place on the work they do, bonds them as a team, and builds their confidence as they implement the information they receive.

Watch for training events that come to your community. Several national youth ministry organizations offer expert training through one-day or weekend workshops that occur in most of the major centers around the nation. They are usually quite affordable and your team will benefit immensely from the cutting edge material they present. Another possibility is to check with a local college or seminary to find youth ministry courses that your key volunteers could audit. Auditing fees are substantially lower than tuition, and your people will receive the same high-quality training that the other students in the class are paying much more for. Also, keep your eyes open for published youth ministry training curriculum produced by youth ministry organizations and denominational youth offices. These packages usually come with a video segment, a leader's guide, and a participant's manual and reduce the stress involved in putting together good material. Another strategy is to have some of your veteran volunteers mentor the rookies. This acknowledges the expertise that has been developed over years of doing

Top-Notch Training Topics for Your Team

★ Youth ministry philosophy

★ Listening/people-helping skills

★ Leading discussions

★ Shaping a lesson

★ How to lead worship

★ Working with parents

★ Youth culture and the media

★ Basics of adolescent development

★ Small group leadership

★ Personal spiritual growth

★ How to share their faith

youth ministry and gives the newly recruited volunteer a supporter who understands what's required to do well in ministry.

When you do schedule meetings with your volunteers, whether for training or planning, make sure that the tone is positive, lively, and encouraging. And make sure that you honor the value of their time by starting promptly and ending your meeting when you promised it would be over.

THANK THEM OFTEN

Working with teenagers can be lonely, thankless work. One of the first books ever written on the subject of youth ministry volunteers was aptly named *Unsung Heroes* (written by Les Christie, published by Zondervan, 1987). The title says it all. Unless, of course, you as a leader make it your mission to let your volunteer leaders know how valued and appreciated they are. Obviously, the easiest way to do this is to simply speak words of encouragement every time they show up at an event or you see them spending quality time with the students. But it's not just face-to-face encouragement that goes a long way. A well-timed text message sent on the evening the small group is meeting can be highly motivational to someone who is making a significant sacrifice for the sake of God's kingdom. An appreciation banquet, perhaps served by some of the students or parents, is a way of letting volunteers know their contribution is valued. Make the evening fun by giving goofy awards to each of them, acknowledging the uniqueness of their personal investment.

One of the most significant ways to provide affirmation is to do so publicly. A "youth worker of the week" in a newsletter or church bulletin lets everyone know that these people are doing a great job. A commissioning service early on in the school year, in which all volunteers gather as a group to be prayed for and affirmed, is another good way to remind everyone of how important their role is. Remember, teenagers rarely think of saying thank you to the people who serve them as consistently and selflessly as your volunteers do; parents often take for granted the benefit their kids receive in a good youth ministry program. That means that if you don't thank them, perhaps no one will.

TRUTH FROM THE TRENCHES

Working with teenagers can be lonely, thankless work. If you don't thank your volunteers for their sacrifices for the kingdom, perhaps no one will.

BE THEIR PASTOR

Youth ministry volunteers give and give and give. Without someone who's willing to pour back into their lives, all this work can be spiritually and emotionally exhausting. This reality may require you to rethink your ministry role substantially. Most of us got into youth ministry because of our deep love for young people and our desire to serve them. As your team begins to grow, it will become necessary to shift your focus from direct, frontline involvement with teenagers to the care and nurture of your volunteers. In a sense, a good youth ministry leader becomes a shepherd of shepherds. There is great joy in recognizing that the investment we make in the pastoral care of our volunteer team members pays huge dividends in the lives of the students they serve.

ACTION PLAN

★ How can you appropriately stay connected with students as your role transitions to being one of shepherding the shepherds?

Sadly, it doesn't always work out the way it's supposed to. One of the most painful jobs that any leader of volunteers has to do is to ask a team member to step down when it becomes necessary. Because each situation is unique, this process isn't easily reduced to a series of predictable steps, but there are some principles that can help make the task a little more manageable and minimize the damage that is done to both the youth ministry and the individual whose ministry is being terminated.

When the "firing" of this person is precipitated by a blatant violation of standards that were in place to ensure the safety of our young people, or when there is clear evidence of moral failure or serious theological compromise, it is, in one sense, easier to have the conversation. It's when we're dealing with a volunteer who "just doesn't get it," or simply brings the wrong gift set, or demonstrates inappropriate motivation for being involved in the lives of students, that it becomes an especially difficult task.

Of course, many of these confrontations can be avoided by ensuring that the recruitment process is done thoroughly and carefully. Expectations should be communicated clearly and in written form. As we've discussed, reference checks, a probationary period, and thorough training should ensure that the volunteer team is positioned for success in the lives of your young people.

But there are still unfortunate cases where it becomes necessary to have the difficult conversation that ultimately ends in the volunteer's departure from the ministry. One of your goals should be to keep the entire process redemptive. Termination should be viewed as a last, reluctant step. Although simply letting someone go may be the quickest way to solve a problem, it is generally not the most loving way. Before that final step is taken ask yourself these questions:

★ Has this person been appropriately trained, empowered, and resourced to do their job effectively? Have we positioned them for success?

★ Is there a role within our youth ministry that would be better suited to this person's gifts, passions, abilities, or schedule? If not, what about another ministry department in the church?

★ Is this person simply burned out and in need of a break or sabbatical?

★ Have I had an honest conversation with this individual that has clearly and lovingly communicated the gap between expectations and performance and my willingness to help them improve?

★ How can the conversation about termination communicate care for the individual and appreciation for their willingness to have served as a volunteer?

★ Is there a way to do this that will minimize feelings of shame, personal failure, and embarrassment? How will I ensure that their dignity is honored?

The tone that is set when these questions are asked, and answered, can ensure that the decision being made is for the sake of the volunteer and not simply for the convenience or ease of the leader. These conversations are always difficult; you can usually count on there being some sort of damage to everyone involved—the leader, the volunteer, the rest of the team. Even our students are often impacted by these decisions. This is why we place such a high emphasis on thoughtful recruitment, careful screening, thorough training, and regular evaluation.

TRUTH FROM THE TRENCHES

The tone that is set when meeting with a volunteer who is being taken off the ministry team should always be one that has the volunteer's best in mind and not simply one that facilitates the convenience or ease of the leader.

FINAL THOUGHTS

Volunteers in ministry offer their most precious gift when they serve. They give themselves. The leader who fails to recognize the incredible value of this gift and takes for granted the willingness of team members to serve misunderstands the economy of God's kingdom. Leadership begins with humility and gratitude. Paul's words to his friends in Philippi are an apt way to wrap things up.

If you've got anything at all out of following Christ, if his love has made any difference in your life, if being in a community of the Spirit means anything to you, if you have a heart, if you care—then do me a favor: Agree with each other, love each other, be deep-spirited friends. Don't push your way to the front; don't sweet-talk your way to the top. Put yourself aside, and help others get ahead. Don't be obsessed with getting your own advantage. Forget yourselves long enough to lend a helping hand. Think of yourselves the way Christ Jesus thought of himself.

PHILIPPIANS 2:1-5, *The Message*

When leaders model this attitude, volunteers will follow and the students we serve together will see a live demonstration of the character of Christ. And when it gets down to it, that's what youth ministry is all about.

TRUTH FROM THE TRENCHES

Volunteers in ministry offer their most precious gift when they serve. They give themselves. Your leadership of them should always begin with humility and gratitude.

ACTION PLAN

★ In what ways can you more deeply model humility and gratitude for your leadership team?

MAKING IT WORK BY BUILDING SUCCESSFUL, HAPPY TEAMS

★ Look again at the relationships of Jesus and his disciples. What are some lessons we can learn about functioning as a healthy team and leading well?

★ What are the inevitable outcomes you would expect to see when a leader fails to eliminate a team member who needs to go?

★ Think of at least five creative and meaningful ways to affirm or say thank you to the volunteers who work on your team.

★ After reading this book, what are the three most important things you can change that will help you build and mobilize your team?

APPENDIX 1
SAMPLE VOLUNTEER
ROLE DESCRIPTION

First Community Church
Cross-Walk Youth Ministries
Junior High Small Group Leader

Role Overview

To provide hospitality, relational availability, biblical instruction, and spiritual guidance to a group of six to ten junior high guys or girls through a scheduled weekly small group time and other informal interactions.

Duties and Responsibilities

★ Develop a personal relationship with each student in the small group
★ Pray for each student in the group regularly
★ Open your home to students for the evening of the small group meeting
★ Provide a simple snack for the evening; examples: juice and cookies or fruit
★ Prepare and lead small group Bible study from provided curriculum
★ Connect informally with three to four students each week; examples: phone calls, Facebook exchange, conversations at church, Coke dates, etc.
★ Attend planning and training meetings as scheduled

Qualifications and Requirements

★ Completed full application and screening process
★ Six-month history of regular attendance at the church
★ Completed the church's Small Group Leaders Training Program

Lines of Communication

★ Classified as youth ministry volunteer staff; report directly to the youth pastor

Training, Support, and Resources Provided

★ Orientation and training prior to beginning the role
★ Mentoring relationship with one of the veteran small group leaders for the first year
★ Curriculum and all teaching supplies
★ $1 per week per participant to help with snack expenses
★ Open door access to the youth pastor as needed
★ Annual evaluation and feedback with the youth pastor
★ Substitute leader available with 24-hour notice
★ Child care provided for all training and planning events

Commitment Required

★ Four to five hours weekly for preparation and hosting of the Bible Study
★ Two hours weekly for informal interactions with students
★ Three training events per year—one full Saturday, two evenings
★ Commit for one year at a time
★ Small groups run from September to May with two weeks off at Christmas

APPENDIX 2
YOUTH MINISTRY VOLUNTEER INITIAL APPLICATION FORM

By filling out this form accurately and honestly you are helping our church provide a safe and caring environment for every young person we serve. Thanks for your willingness to explore the possibility of joining our team.

Name ....

Spouse's name ....

Address ....

Daytime phone ....

Mobile ....

E-mail address..................................

SSN ....

Date of birth ....

Circle the words or phrases that the people who know you best would use to describe you:

Relatively free of personal problems; Emotionally intelligent; Authentic; Loving; Encouraging; Flexible; Faithful; Examined life; Creative; Teachable; Integrity; Visionary; Enthusiastic; Natural leadership ability; Energetic; Servant-hearted; Sense of humor

Do you consider our church to be your home church? ❑Yes ❑No If no, where do you attend?

....

....

What other areas of church life are you actively involved in?..............................

....

....

List all previous ministry or leadership experience: ....

....

....

....

....

....

Please respond to the following questions as thoroughly as you can.

1. What are the highlights of your spiritual journey to date?

....

....

2. What are some of the strengths you'll bring to the youth ministry team?

....

....

3. Where will you need to be supported in your ministry because of personal weaknesses or vulnerabilities you are aware of? ....

....

....

4. Are there any issues in your past that we should be aware of that might impact your role as a leader of young people? ....

....

....

Please provide three references who can speak to your character, spiritual maturity, work ethic, and temperament. ....

....

Thanks! If you have any questions about this process, please feel free to call (<u>Your Name</u>) at (<u>Your Number</u>).

MARV'S PICKS: MORE GREAT RESOURCES ON BUILDING & MOBILIZING EFFECTIVE TEAMS

David Chow, *No More Lone Rangers: New Ideas on How to Build a Team-Centered Youth Ministry* (Loveland, CO: Group Publishing, 2002)

Les Christie, *How to Recruit and Train Volunteer Youth Workers: Reaching More Kids with Less Stress* (Grand Rapids: Zondervan, 1992)

Doug Fields, *Help! I'm a Volunteer Youth Worker: 50 Easy Tips to Help You Succeed with Kids* (Grand Rapids: Zondervan/Youth Specialties, 2001)

Doug Fields, *Your First Two Years in Youth Ministry: A Personal and Practical Guide to Starting Right* (Grand Rapids: Zondervan/Youth Specialties, 2002)

Kurt Johnston, *Middle School Ministry Made Simple* (Cincinnati: Standard Publishing, 2008)

John Maxwell, *The 17 Indisputable Laws of Teamwork: Embrace Them and Empower Your Team* (Nashville: Thomas Nelson, 2001)

Ginny Olson, Diane Elliot, and Mike Work, *Youth Ministry Management Tools: Everything You Need to Successfully Manage Your Ministry* (Grand Rapids: Zondervan/Youth Specialties, 2001)

Patrick Snow, *Leading Preteens* (Cincinnati: Standard Publishing, 2007)

Andy Stanley, *Next Generation Leader: Five Essentials for Those Who Will Shape the Future* (Sisters, OR: Multnomah Books, 2006).

MORE ABOUT MARV
(THAN YOU WANTED TO KNOW)

Marv Penner has been in youth ministry longer than most youth workers have been alive. His ministry journey started as a bullhorn-toting, guitar-playing program director at a summer camp in the early '70s. It wasn't long before he was the youth pastor of a rapidly growing church in Toronto, where he spent thirteen years on the pastoral team. He's taught at colleges and seminaries around the world for the past twenty years while maintaining a private counseling practice with deeply hurting kids.

Marv is the author of a half-dozen books on youth ministry, including *Youth Worker's Guide to Parent Ministry* and *Hope and Healing for Kids Who Cut.*

He has taught thousands of youth workers in dozens of countries as part of the Youth Specialties speaking team for more than fifteen years, and continues to serve international youth workers every chance he gets. Marv serves on the Understanding Your Teenager team and is an associate staff member with the Center for Parent/Youth Understanding.

Marv loves his empty nest life with his wife, Lois. Canoe trips, motorcycle touring, nature photography, and travel to out-of-the-way places are a few of the things that keep them from getting bored. Marv and Lois have three grown children who have each married well. Grandchildren are just now beginning to arrive.

Learn more about Marv's ministry at www.yscanada.com.